A Boy in Tetbury

Contents

Many Thanks ....

Just a note v

The first Part - A Sort of Dream 1

The second Part - The Streets of Tetbury and some people 2

Long Street 2

The Town Hall .... .10

Back Down Long Street .... .12

Church Street .... .21

The Other Side of Church Street .... .27

Silver Street and Fox Hill .... .30

Chipping Street .... .32

The Chipping .... .33

Chipping Steps .... .37

Gumstool Hill .... .39

Market Place .... .41

Cirencester Road .... .44

New Church Street .... .45

Coombers Mead and Gashouse Row .... .47

West Street .... .48

Bath Road .... .54

Hampton Street .... .57

The Third Part - Living at Upton Road 58

The Fourth Part - A Working Boy 88

The Fifth Part - Family Matters 99

My Sisters 104

My Brothers 109

The Sixth Part - My Career 113

Pegler's Man 113

The Seventh Part - The Rest of Tetbury 139

Witchell's 139

Some More Tetbury People 144

Children and Babies 163

A Country Boy 165

The Eighth Part - the Rest of my Career 174

Ninth Part - Away from Tetbury 183

Shipton Moyne Relations - Peters and Vizor 183

Going to Malmesbury 197

Long Newnton 200

The Wider World 201

The Church and the Brethren 203

What Happened in Hull 210

Motorbike and Sidecar 215

Many thanks

A lot of people have helped to put the book together. I would like to thank my brother, David Peters, and my sister, Ann Moss (always referred to in the book as 'Elizabeth Ann') for their help in going over long stretches of the manuscript with Dad, reading it out to him when he found that even reading was difficult, and making notes.

I have to thank my cousin, Pat Maybrey, the archivist of the Vizor family, for checking a number of details which were otherwise vague or Dad's guesses.

The staff of the Gloucestershire County Record Office were particularly helpful.

Many of the illustrations of Tetbury before the first world war were supplied by Julian Pearce of Hampton Street, Tetbury. I cannot thank him enough. They include photographs by Jimmy Clark, ET Lamb, and Mr Williams of New Church Street. At least two of Julian's pictures were 'missing' family ones.

Other pictures were taken by David Peters and Cliff Moss, Ann's husband; John Cull, the grandson of Jesse Cull in the book, provided one; my cousin Grace Harper (née Hills, once of Long Newnton as well as Long Street) provided another. We found several at home that had been taken by Persis Lamb for Council publications. The picture of Gale's shop was taken by George Gale and is used by permission of Mr M Gale of Porthleven, Cornwall. Johnny-in-the-Morning is in the Gloucestershire County Records Office collection. The photograph of Mrs Dance came from the Ted Prince/HOTS collection. Special thanks, too, to Jeff Bird, churchwarden, and the St Mary's Church archive, for the ET Lamb picture of the church interior.

I had helpful advice from some Tetbury shopkeepers, and from members of the History of Tetbury Society, as well as from members of the Nailsworth Local History Research Group, especially my cousin Nick Peters.

I must mention DavesDiscDoctor for rescuing most of the text when the old Amstrad gave up, and transferring it onto Mac-friendly floppies.

Finally I thank my wife, Myra, for putting up with the project for so long, for making many helpful suggestions, and for proofreading everything several times over.

John Peters

A Boy in Tetbury

Just a note

When he was ninety years old my father, Frank Peters, began to write the story of his life. He told me that he had often thought about doing it, but it had taken him a long time to get started. Unfortunately he found that the actual writing had become too hard. He said, 'I should have started this years ago.'

I offered to help him by recording his story and writing it up from tapes. When I had grasped his style we continued by taking notes face to face, or over the telephone as he was living in Yorkshire at that time and I was in London.

As soon as a few transcripts appeared he wanted to edit them. 'No,' he would say, 'that's quite wrong!' The result is that the final version is different from the surviving tapes. But most of the editing is his: I moved things around into the 'Parts' as they now are and added a name or a phrase to indicate who somebody was. A great deal of time had to be spent in the Gloucestershire County Record Office tracking down voters' lists and school registers to discover exactly how people spelled their names*. Often, the name had a spelling that we did not expect.

Dad wanted illustrations, and we began to look through photograph albums and other family archives. People who knew what he was doing began to lend us their own pictures. One or two that he specially wanted have disappeared from view though in most cases substitutes have been found.

By the end of 1999 the story was almost complete but he was often ill the following year, and the work slowed down to a crawl. We agreed his final version of the text in August 2000.

In September that year he died, suddenly though not unexpectedly. The family agreed that we should go ahead with his book.

A Boy in Tetbury is Frank's own story. It may be inaccurate in parts; it isn't supposed to be an authentic history of Tetbury; it covers a very limited time, mainly between 1905, especially the first few years, and 1930, when he left Tetbury to find a job, with a few pages of other material.

It is a record of a time which is almost but not quite modern, and a place which is almost but not quite recognisable, a Tetbury where most people had some allegiance to some church or other; where there was a 'rich' C of E church and a 'poor' one; where there were two varieties of Baptist church, two of Methodist and two of Plymouth Brethren as well as Congregational, all well attended, perhaps except by 'the drinking people', as Frank used to call them.

I am proud that I have helped to produce his book.

John Peters, Stonehouse, Gloucestershire

January 2002

*NB As far as I know, all names are spelled correctly: the one anomaly is that Edith Metcalf's mother was Annie Metcalfe, but that was George Metcalfe's fault.

– THE FIRST PART –

A Sort of Dream

I had a load of manure delivered. It's in my front garden, doing good. Pooh! what a smell! But it's a lovely smell for those that like it. It reminds me of living in the country.

I had a sort of dream the other day, that I was going round Tetbury on my calls (as a baker, you know) and when I got to Northfield there wasn't anyone there I knew. Everyone I called on, I said 'How is so and so?' and they said 'They're gone, you know.'

There was the carpenter, and the builder, and the man we sold the dog to, and Eric Vick and his sister Gladys, the butchers from London Road. I got to another house and I said 'How is Fred Bond?' and they said 'Oh, he's been dead a long time!'; and I asked about Phil Potts, who was Fred's pal. They used to ride motorbikes together.

'Oh, he's been gone a long time, too!'

'Gone?'

'Yes, Phil's dead, too!'

I couldn't stop giggling at this. I felt glad, and then I felt sad. I thought, I'd better get out of here!

When I was young in Tetbury I knew everybody. And now there's nobody to be seen. Not even relatives.

In that day I saw everything, and everybody's movements. It's the only thing I was ever good at and it's a bit of a gift. I always used to be able to find things in the house that had been lost or mislaid. I would say 'It's about so high up....' because I had an idea where I had seen it. I always observed things.

– THE SECOND PART –

The Streets of Tetbury and some people

LONG STREET

I knew everyone in Long Street, all the shops and the people. Well, in Long Street Purnell's was the Plough. That's the beginning of Long Street. The pub had a plough sign on it. The first time I saw them using gold lettering was the name of the pub and George Holborow did it himself. The sign was taken down from the top of the building when it stopped being a pub.

The police station was next. There are a lot of stories about the police station - you know Sergeant Woolford's bike is still there? It's a great big bike with an extra crossbar because he was such a big man. When the second war was fully on and there was a blackout the Police Station didn't think anything would ever happen and the lights were shining.

One day a man murdered someone in a field and he wanted to go to the police and tell them. The only policeman he could find was the Sergeant, and he was on point duty by the Town Hall. He went up to the Sergeant and told him what he had done and the Sergeant said 'Get off with you!'

Sergeant Woolford had a daughter called Louie. She would go up to the Picket Harp and steal all the vegetables she wanted, and she never got into any trouble. Everyone knew she did it, and people must have seen her, but nothing ever happened.

There were only two policemen in Tetbury at that time, Sergeant Woolford and one other. They lived in two houses in Hampton Street in the same row as Mr Webb, the School Master. One day they were both working in their front gardens. I thought meself, Someone could be running away with the town!

There was a car accident in the middle of Fox Hill once, and the Sergeant went down to it because he was the only policemen on duty at the time. He was the new sergeant, not Woolford, and a woman had got smashed up. Well, he officiated at the scene and did really well. Then he went back to the station and fell down flat - he fainted away. He was a decent man, and I think he married my father's cousin.

Next to the police station there was Maurice Pride's. He was the solicitor, and my parents thought that he did us out of some money. Let's be telling you this: there's a story about when he had fifty pounds. He told me at the start. He said, 'When I had fifty pounds, when I made fifty pounds, I came out into the street and looked up and down the street, and I thought to myself, I've got everything!' You can see what money was like then, can't you?

Mr Fowler had the grocer's shop opposite Gale's with a door that was top half and bottom half. That was a very long time ago! Then that was Pegler's, and he had a bakehouse there. There's a lot to be said about them, because a lot of my life was spent with the Peglers. And Corney Mann came next. He was a postman and a boot mender, in his house.

And then came what they called the Garret, the Long Street Room where the Open Brethren met and where I went to Sunday School classes. It was next door to Lewis the baker. It belonged to him but he didn't go there. We children had to go there, to the Sunday School, whether we wanted to or not. My father wouldn't go to church at all, he said 'Because I can't hear!'

Lewis the baker always had a good shop, and his grandfather, too, for donkeys' years. Mr Pegler worked for him before he started his own business. I don't know the grandfather but I can show you where he is, because in the churchyard where he is there's a column, broken off, representing the breaking off of his life. He got some corn in his ear. Fancy things like that! That killed him, evidently. That was the grandfather. In my time Alec Lewis was the boss. He wasn't a real baker. He had been in some office before. He married Dorothy McCracken from Scotland. She was a teacher at the infants' school.

After that came the Methodist church, opposite the woman we went to live with once, Mrs Lamb, at Porch House.

After that it was Harry Barnes, another postman. They had to have a lot of postmen, you know. He was a friend of Dad's, not that I knew him or liked him or anything like that, and he had a plot at the Picket Harp, where all the men had plots. He used to keep bees. One of them stung me, but he said 'It wasn't my bee that stung you!'

Then next was Kitcat's office. He was a solicitor, too, with the iron railings round the door, of Paul & Kitcat. Mr Paul was a solicitor but he wasn't somebody I knew: I only found out who he was, but I did know the Kitcats. They lived in a house, The Retreat, with a lane leading up to it on London Road, and Mrs Kitcat bought a pony from someone I can tell you about. Mr Kitcat had a story about a man who came to him and told him he had lost his axe 'in the water'.

'Why, where is it?'

'In the pond.'

'Why then, you know where it is. It isn't lost!'

After that there's a big house called The Ferns and that was a lady, a family of gentry as they call them. It became the Grammar School, but I think that was more something at the back. Grace went to that school, Olive's daughter, and her brother Douglas.

Then there's the big shop, Harris, clothes and all that; and then came the saddler with the fox in the window. I think that's all gone. And then

The big shop, Harris in Long Street, was a department store. You can see the list of departments in the upstairs window.

next to it was still the same people, the husband of the big shop, and the son - they kept a cycle shop - Aubrey Fowles, where I didn't buy a motor bike from. Because the simple reason was, there he was talking in the room with his father, in the shop, and I only had my bank book to go to the Post Office, like a big man. I wanted one of those little black Ariels, a motor bicycle. Anyrate I didn't buy it because, do you know, I got incensed. They went on chattering and I thought, No, you don't mind! When they could see me there and I had to wait, and I had the money to spend on him. Anyrate, I thought, That's the lot! That's the limit! and I went on my way and I didn't buy it. Funny story, isn't it! No, I didn't buy the bike. There wasn't anywhere else in Tetbury to get a new motorbike, and that one was in the window and it met my eye.

Then we have Godwin's shop, an electrician, and next to that was Clancy's, the people that had the theatre at the White Hart Hotel. The hotel ballroom came to be a theatre.

Mr. Pitman, who taught me at Sunday School and ran the boys' cricket team, worked at Braine's the tailors in Long Street. To the right of Braine's is Wright's, with a sunblind, the printer's and newsagent's shop where I took the Wilts and Gloster Standard out, among other jobs; then the Ormond's Head with its glass canopy, and then Robert Street's garage.

Edith took the children to Lawn's to have their hair cut. I helped my sister Olive and her family when they moved from a house in Long Newnton to the flat above the shop.

Then after that there was the famous shop where I went to take the newspapers out, called Wright's, the printers. My first job there was to take all the printing rubbish from the printshop to the scavenge heap at the Herd. On Friday evening I had another job: I went there to deliver the Wilts and Gloster Standard. And on Saturday I went back to Wright's to clean the shop. They had a machine, like you've seen, for cutting lots of paper together. I put a stick under their machine and it cut it in two. There's another story here: once I found some money under a great mat while I was cleaning, and I gave it to them. But it happened once or twice more and I thought I had better arrest them with it, and I told them 'If

I find any more I shall keep it.' I earned one and six a week there.

Now then, after that is the pub they call the Ormond's Head: poor old Eddie used to spend some time in there. They had a window that came down, sash windows they call them, and there they would be in there. All the smoke! You could look through the window but you couldn't see who was there for the smoke, but Eddie would be in amongst them. He was a joiner, as they call it - he went and joined them.

Then after that the next thing was Lawn's the hairdresser. They did ladies' and children's hair. It wasn't Lawn's then, it was another shop, it was a foreign person. It was a stone built house, standing up two or three flights. My sister Olive, when she got married, she lived in one of the flats.

After that it's Robert Street's. Now, Robert Street's was a big place and it extended to his house, but that was a garage. Now it's one of those big stores, Gateway Stores. Robert Street's house was next to the garage, and the first time I went home with my wife - I don't know if we were married then - we had a big surprise, because we simply didn't know many people. But he knew me, because I used to go in there for Pegler's van. He said 'Hello, Mr Peters,' and then I sort of introduced Edith. He told me how pleased he was: 'How nice to see me' - and he was real nice.

After I had spent nineteen shillings on my bicycle, putting on new pedals or something - nineteen shillings! that was a lot of money that day! - I went to work early and Eddie went to work at eight, and he always used to pinch my bike. I got on to him once or twice and nothing happened. My mother said to me (she thought I was a millionaire - I don't know where I saved it, that's the trouble, but I did - I had some money) 'Look here, Frank.' She said 'If you buy Eddie a bicycle, when he has to pay you, I'll see that he pays you.' So we did that. That cost five pounds. A Hercules bike. Beautiful. It would be a good bike even now. Better than they've got now, do you know, which if anything went wrong they wouldn't know what to do with all those gears, would they? No, it would have to cost them I don't know how much.

I got the bicycle for Eddie from Robert Street. He put me a pump in, too. A new bike for Eddie. Well, then he never used mine. He did pay me back. Oh yes, he had to. Oh, he would do that, with being commanded by his mother to do it.

Past Robert Street's house there's a shop that was owned by two ladies then, White and Upton, a sweet shop. When I was there with Cliff, my daughter's husband, I stood outside this shop, and I said, 'In 1924, as a boy, I was standing here looking up the street like this to watch the first electric light come on in the town. The first electric light! It was on the streets and it came on at the top of the town against the corner, going down Church Street, on the corner.'

There was only one light, about a forty watt bulb! Oh, that's right, about a forty watt bulb, but anyrate that's by the by. I thought myself, By grums! some of the gas lights we've got are better than that, aren't they surely? We'd got gas lights in the street, you see. Incidentally, there was no pipe in the earth for the gas. It had been so long in the earth when they altered the lighting. They were working outside Pegler's (where I worked then) when they got done with the gas. They were searching for a pipe and all there was left was a hole going all up the road. No wonder it smelled. But anyrate - that was outside Pegler's. I had Cliff up there by the sweet shop, and it's funny how you mark one thing. I said 'The light came on and this is where I stood like the rest of everybody else, of course. As a kid.' It's funny, ain't it?

We're outside the sweet shop, oh yes, and I'll tell you what happened. When we had finished talking about the electric light, I turned round to the sweet shop and there was a list as long as your leg, CUT PRICE, and do you know what it was? It was cigarettes, and the cheapest was two pound for a packet! I says to Cliff 'How much are they, then?'

He said 'There you are!'

I said 'I used to get mine for tuppence and fourpence and sixpence! I got the best at sixpence - BDV and all the brands practically for sixpence! Now they are all two pound something!' and I said to him 'Aren't you glad you don't smoke?' It was terrible. Bit of a lark, you know.

The next shop was the ironmonger's, Munday and Fowler (not Monday and Tuesday). Mrs Munday and Dorothy at the bakehouse, the young woman who was the schoolteacher, at Lewises the bakers, used to put together for a painting competition and I used to win. I got the prize each year for that. It was fifteen shillings. I used to win the painting competition. Tis funny, isn't it?

This picture of Tetbury Carnival procession must have been taken from the Market House. I am not sure what year it was, but our family was always in the procession. I don't recognise her, but the girl dressed as Britannia was called Molly.

That used to be at Tetbury Carnival. Our family always did a lot for the carnival. I won a prize for fancy dress several times. Once I went as Little Boy Blue, and another time I went as All You Can Eat For Ninepence, all covered up with food. I remember I had a loaf that was specially made for me!

Munday and Fowler had a lot of workmen, but not one was any good to them for doing what my father did. That is, case hardening tools. There was no more equipment for working on the roads than a pickaxe, a shovel, and a barrow, and that's how everything was conducted. Now, there wasn't even a handbarrow with two wheels for anything, and men used to carry a bag of flour away from Tetbury on their shoulder, or two bags of flour. How far would it be? Right up to Beverstone, or Chavenage House. There was never any roadmaking tools other than that. Now, I look round and see there's earth removers, they remove the earth, don't they, let alone dig a trench!

The first thing that came around was like a tractor that went into the hole and went along and as it turned out it was like a shoveller. Nothing was ever changed until after the first world war, nothing. My dad's special job was sharpening the pickaxes, by the fire and in the fire. He hammered them, and that. There was him and his brother Walter then, and both of them were dab hands at doing this job. There was all Munday and Fowler's and their fellows had to come to Dad and his brother Walter at Witchell's and ask them for case hardened tools.

Well, that's all that side of Long Street except for Fawkes' and Gillott's, both grocers, under the Penthouse, and Butler's the butcher's shop, a high class place. There was the hardware place and the butcher's and then Gillot's the grocers and then Fawkes'. Gillot's is Cirencester. Fawkes' was a grocer's, too. Fawkes's tea was called Ambaflo. When I pour my tea out now I say 'Ambaflo'; I say 'We'll have a drop of Ambaflo.'

In the war Jim Pegler would go up from his bakehouse to Gillotts and buy an extra box of fat - lard or suchlike - from them, because they couldn't get enough. It was rationed. I suppose it was Gillott's to sell and they sold it to him.

When I was working for The Priory, I went into the butcher's, when I had to do such as this: I took a calf, a bull calf, to be killed for veal, and I had to hold the calf while Mr Wilkins killed it. He just held the gun there and BOOM. That just happened once.

It's ever so funny: what they did then at butchers' shops was to go up to their field and drive all the cattle down. There was a space where they could keep them in, standing by them, and somebody would come out and pick what they wanted out of them. To kill. Do you know, they found it a difficulty to get the cattle to come up to that place? They seemed to know. That's ever so queer, isn't it? They seemed to know something.

THE TOWN HALL

They used to use the Town Hall, the Market House at the top of Long Street, for all the business of the town. They used to keep the fire engine there in a sort of box, a part of the building made purposely for it. There was a market under the arches, and when there wasn't a market all the unemployed men used to hang around there. When the cinema caught fire all the men from under the arches held the hose to let the water go free; and to get it high, so that they could pour water on the flames, they got a ladder and a man climbed up with the hose, and all the others hanging on below.

The firemen were all volunteers and had another job. I remember the first fire engine: it was hand operated and manned by two men one side and two men the other. That is, it was pumped by hand, two men a side. They used to practise pumping with it at the New Pool. They always tried to get enough pressure to make the water shoot up in the air, but they got tired. But they emptied the New Pool.

One of them was my friend Arthur Barrett who lived on the way down to the station in Fox Hill. I've seen him holding the hosepipe. He always had a piece of cigarette in his mouth; it wouldn't be more than an inch long. He had the hose in both hands - you would think he would have burned his mouth.

He was one who hung around under the Town Hall all day long. He never had any work. Arthur Barrett could do any sums in his head, but he couldn't do anything else. When he was at school I remember he would pop his hand up and answer the teacher. He was good at sums but nothing else. When he left school he got a job as a cowman, but he lost that, and when he was unemployed he walked up and down under the Town Hall. He was a magician with figures, but that's all he knew.

It was a horse-drawn fire engine, and they used the horses that pulled the wagons for Warn's Brewery if they had to go to a fire outside the town.

I remember once in the summer someone was saying 'There's all this carn a-burnin!' The fires were often on farms. It was always a ride to get to them, and if the brewery was doing a delivery they had to wait for Warn's horses to come back before they could take the engine out. When this chap said about the 'carn' someone else said 'Back in an hour!'

One day there was a fire at a gentleman's house about two miles away. It was when I was a chimney sweep. I was on my motorbike going up the road towards our house when a man came out and stopped me. 'Are you very busy?' he said.

'Not particularly,' I said.

'Well, will you take me to the fire?'

'All right. You'll have to sit on the box.' That was where I kept all the sweep's equipment, like a sidecar. So he got up on the box of the bike and off we went. That was how the firemen used to get to a fire in those days - get a lift from somebody!

Well, when we got there I was an important man, because they quickly put the fire out, and then the firemen had to get home. They asked me to wait for my man until it was all over and the man of the house said it would be hard on us to go home hungry, so we all had some food - in the hand, you know, not sitting down - and then I took my fireman back to Tetbury.

Tetbury fire brigade in those days was enough to make a cat laugh!

There was nothing sold in the Tetbury shops when I was a little boy. For instance, nobody sold tomatoes before the first world war. People grew most of their food except for bread, cheese and meat. In fact, Tetbury was a poor, shabby sort of place that had nothing.

But on market day there were all sorts of stalls under the Market House. You could get a big piece of fish for sixpence. We liked that. Or we had rock salmon for one shilling and sixpence a pound from the man who came there from Stroud. Fishy Williams, who kept the fish shop, he came later. There used to be butchers' stalls there, and the pub across the road at the back was the Jolly Butchers. There was another pub as well behind the market, called the Boot, but I don't remember anyone selling boots in the market. Everything else came later, after the war.

BACK DOWN LONG STREET

On the right hand side of Long Street, by the Market House, there was Mr Gething, the man that kept the corner house. Do you know how he came to Tetbury? You know, with a banjo! Singing! but he had education I suppose, and he never had a job, and he got that one. The old man, Clark, died - I'd known him for years and years - and it was a sweet shop then. And a toy shop. All locked in there with shutters. Gething took it on.

The top of Long Street – we used to call it 'the top of the town'. The last shop on the right was the butcher.

Jimmy Clark sold toys from this shop at the corner of Long Street and Church Street. He was a very good photographer, and took several of the photographs in the book. Mr Gething had the shop after him. You can see part of a crossing swept through the horse droppings across Long Street, in front of the policeman.

Not half the list of Tetbury. There's plenty. Let's start again where Gething was and go back down Long Street. There was a big bank, I don't remember which one, but Rene kept her money there, and it used to be part of Prouts Stores. Prouts was a shoe and clothes shop, as well as a proper grocer's shop. The fellow that worked for the grocer would have to take anything on his bike, whether it was a bag of sugar or a side of bacon, to deliver it to the customers. There was usually so much on that he couldn't get off the bike without falling off.

One man built that bank, a man named Sparrow. I suppose he liked a drop of ale. Give him plenty of drink and he would do all of it. And his eyes were right hanging down there.

Not a car in sight! Macdonald's was a very modern garage and bodyshop. You can see they sold Pratts Spirit. Cars went upstairs on a lift. My next door neighbour George Medcroft worked there. There has been a gap in Long Street ever since Macdonalds was demolished.

There was Macdonald's Garage, too, that's where there's a piece left out of Long Street altogether, where there's a gap. All the vehicles used to be lifted up into there and go in there upstairs, lots of them. It was wonderful! Anyrate, that's it. They were carriage builders and they did carriages for horses as well. Anything that needed painting, they painted it, more or less, including carts. George Medcroft, Goggy, used to be a painter for them there, painting cars. It was called Macdonald's Coach and Motor Works and Garage. Now it's a VIP petrol station, a great big hole in the street.

A lot of the houses in Long Street have been altered by taking the plaster off. They alter things. The Americans took over one of those buildings during the war. It may have been Macdonald's. I'll tell you something about the Americans: when they went for their dinner they used to walk out into the street, and they used to be slouching worse than the Italians! If any of our soldiers came around, they would sort of square up and they would Quick March! em.

Anyrate, then there was Richard Holborow's grocer's shop, not greengrocer's. Now, that Holborow was a relative of George Holborow the big builder. A little quality grocer's, high class. There were some steps to get down. We never bought much from them. Frank Bird used to work for Holborows in the grocers. He was the errand boy, and he used to ride about Tetbury with sides of bacon on his bike. He was as strong as a lion. He was one who went gleaning wheat with us.

Then of course, Colonel Morrison-Bell come next, at The Close. Old friend. Colonel Morrison-Bell's wife was a real lady, a friend to Edith, and she would be daughter to the people who lived in the house where the Prince is, Highgrove. Colonel Morrison Bell's wife entertained Edith at The Close.

Then after that came Lloyds bank. After Lloyds Bank there came the chemist's shop, Freddie Evans. When Gilbert Pegler was a young man, he went in for a tooth to the chemist. You see there was no dentist in the place then, and Freddie Evans and the like would drag teeth - pull one out for you. He was only as big as a threepenny bit was Freddie Evans. You would come in and he took you in the back room. Gilbert went in and Freddie Evans started pulling away and the doorbell rang and he went into the shop to serve the people: 'Back in a minute!' He came back to have another go. It was a murderous job! This is not untrue. This is true. Truly, I mean you think sometimes that some things are real abominable.

I think the greengrocer's shop further down belonged to Holborow, and there is a story connected to Peglers and some rhubarb, but it's a long way round to tell you this story, and it comes in the right place, later on, with the story about working for Pegler. Next to Holborow's there was little Mrs Pride. Her husband, Charlie Pride, was a baker who used to work for Lewises. They lived between Freddie Evans and the greengrocer.

'Charlie! Charlie! Come unto these boys! They be quarling!' (that was Mrs Pride).

'We baint, our Dad! Our hands be perfectly still!' (that was the Pride boys).

The youngest boy had the stick at school every day for coming in late. It didn't cure him. They were called Charlie, who was the eldest, Penis and Teddy, and there was a sister. The middle one, well, they couldn't have known what they were calling him! They used to shout for him. You can't imagine it, can you?

The Prides were some relation to Mother, but what degree I don't think I ever knew. They used to go to the Congregational Church in The Chipping, and the sister was going to be married, and the minister, who was a very old man, tried to marry two other people.

There's only one more house in between that and the barber's, and I don't know that anyone was living in it when I was working for Pegler. It used to be Francis Lewis, a retired builder. He moved to The Green. Then it came to the barber's shop. When we were in the barber's shop in that day, we had to pay tuppence for a haircut, and he knew enough from the kids like us, what he wanted to know - everything, see! How I got on with the Peglers, and all that kind of thing! Proper, proper news-bag, he was! John Shepphard, his name was, the father of the John Shepphard who came later. That's who I'm talking about. His shop was on the left-hand side, where the pavement goes out.

Now then, here's another story: I met a boy there, a boy from the end of the street, down at the bottom, Guy Holland he was called. He had a ten-shilling note in his hand, and he was coming up Long Street, playing with it, acting the fool with it. When he was outside that shop he let it go and the wind blew it up, and blew it over the house and something happened - very mercifully because he would have got skinned for it - it went down, and over the house, and back down into the corner, where I told you. It went round and round and he picked it up! He would have got striped for it because his mother was like that. I carried water for Mrs Holland when Guy wasn't there.

That was her son. I was talking to him once - he had been in the army by then - and he told me a story of being on a charge. According to Guy, he had walked across the Square with a cigarette in his mouth. Well, I think that's what he meant. The way he told it to me was this: 'I was walking across the cigarette with the Square in my mouth!'

Next to the barber's shop was just a private house or two. And who lived there in that time was the people whose grandfather had the shop in The Chipping that became Murray's fish shop. It was a seed shop then. I remember it very well. I believe their name was Young.

Come on, down to Dr Walker; Dr Walker was a real doctor, a fine built man, but he was another of those men that used to pull out teeth without anything - without any anaesthetic. I told you about Freddie Evans. Dr Walker was just the same! There wasn't a dentist about. Of course, all things came after the first world war, and altered. I suppose it did. There came nothing before that. Oh, it was horrible!

Even after the war there was only one proper dentist came to Tetbury and he came sometimes, in a car. One day when he was driving in to work he lost his bag off the back where he had a hood to put up, and it landed in the road and spilled, where Eddie and I found it. It was full of false teeth and instruments - the lot of it. We picked the bits up and took them to the police station. We got a few coppers for it from the police and he had his bag back.

We thought that was a stinking job. If we had hung on to it until it was announced that it was missing we could have taken it back to him and no doubt he would have given us something. We thought the police probably had a touch of the reward.

One time Eddie had the toothache so bad that he got up in the night and took the dog for a walk, right up into Tetbury and round by Chavenage Green, and all around. There wasn't a dentist then apart from the man with the car, though you could go to the doctor or Freddie and have a tooth pulled out.

One time I was working with a fellow with bad teeth and he was frightened of having them out. He wouldn't have anything done to them. He went away from work ill, and he died.

After Dr Walker there were two or three houses, but nothing to talk of. Then there was Porch House. That would be a school then, I should think, and then Council offices. Mrs Lamb lived there, in part of the house, later. There was another school in Silver Street called Benge's School - they were both private schools.

This is one of the photographs Persis Lamb took for Tetbury Council. The left hand side of Porch House was the Council Offices. The right side was Mrs Lamb's house. When we moved back to Tetbury in 1941 and I worked for Pegler again we lived in rooms in the gables on the right.

Then of course, Dr Brodie come next after Mrs Lamb's house, but nobody knows about Dr Brodie because that is so far back; I knew Dr Brodie, but nobody else would - it's one of those things nobody would know now. That's the house called Old House now, but it was called School House then. It was another private school before he had it. The Miss Gales went to school there, and at that time it was called School House. Then Mrs Ormandy's came next and then Cyril that worked with me at Peglers lived in the next house. Cyril Newman.

Mr George Gale took this photograph, not long before I became the errand boy. The famous Gale & Son sign had not been made then.

Then, of course, Gale's. But at first was the sweet shop, Miss Little, where I spent a farthing before going to school and I had a farthing to come back to after school. I was all right for sweets! She was blind, and I have no doubt that children stole things, and how do you think it could pay? I don't understand it at all! Of course, she would buy in bulk of sweets. A farthingsworth of sweets!

Old Mr and Mrs Gale were in the Brethren, and perhaps George Gale was once, but not when I knew him. He sold me my first car when he got a motorbike. He used to go up and down to Cornwall, and he went to live at Brixham in Devon, when he retired.

Miss Little's was next door to Gale's, and her shop came into George Gale's place. When he got married, and the sweet shop ceased, they had that for a home. Even in that day, mind, Gale's shop was a posh place and it's been such a poor tumbledown place, sold rubbish, ever since my brother Raymond left it. It was a first-class grocer's shop that sold everything - everything that gentry wanted. Gale's sent goods round by van - they didn't have one of their own: it belonged to someone else.

They called it their 'outside service', and people could buy what was in the van.

Apart from that they didn't deliver orders themselves, but they got them delivered. They had a good country round. They would make up parcels of groceries for outlandish places and the errand boy would run them to Phillips the baker with a penny on each of them to deliver them when they went round with the bread. Think of it, a penny to deliver the groceries!

It was a right job, that was, when I worked there as an errand boy. Bert Bignell was the errand boy when I was a littleun, and when he left I took over from him.

The ladies used to come in the shop and give their orders to the people behind the counter, and they would offer them a piece of cheese. Now, we always had two half hundredweight cheeses on the counter, beautiful cheeses, nothing like what we have today, and they would get an instrument, a gouge, and dig it into the cheese and take a piece out and the ladies would taste it before they ordered any. The cheeses were covered with a cloth, and it was quite a job to get the cloth off and put it back on again. Well, if there wasn't anybody there, sometimes I was by myself in the shop, and I would uncover the cheese and get the gouge and stick it well in, and come up with a piece of cheese. Then I would break off the inside bit and put the outside bit back in the big cheese and eat the inside bit while I was covering the cheese up again. That was naughty. I never thought anyone would do anything like that!

I used to take out things, take the orders from Gale's up to people's houses. I used to get it on a barrow and push it up to Warn's the brewers in Church Street, where my brother Eddie lived afterwards. Now, everywhere where boys were, we used to trot. Now people do it for fun, and they call it jogging. But everywhere we went, I would trot up there with this package of stuff and get on the job with it, the mouth closed, trotting, and go on. The Warns were a family of very big people and they needed a lot of food. Although they were brewers, they drank a lot of water to swill it down.

I used to go to the bank for Gale's, up Long Street. This is the funniest part. I only took forty pounds! That was the takings! You see, if one man had fifty pounds he was rich! They would be piling in fifty pounds! But of course they were paying out from it as well. Gradually it would get to be something, wouldn't it?

In Gale's there were all kinds of matches, not just ordinary Bryant and Mays and Moreland's England's Glory from Gloucester. They were bigger and uglier than anything you have ever seen.

One day I trotted up from Gale's and went into the bank and I was on fire! because I had had a box of the red topped matches in my pocket - I used to smoke when I was quite a little boy, anything, even old mans beard - and it had ignited as I was trotting along. They were England's Glory matches, most unsafe matches, and Mr Tovey the bank manager said 'What's the matter with you? You're on fire!' and he helped me to put it out. He could have given me five pounds, but he didn't.

He was a great big fellow from Wales (they're not big in Wales, are they?) and he had two big sons. One of them had a Harley Davidson, a beautiful big bike, and he ran into our front railings on it one day and knocked them down. He paid for repairing them of course. But they were all big fellows. Anyrate, that's the story of my job at Gale's.

CHURCH STREET

Mr Montgomery had the watchmaker's shop on the right; next is the Post Office. The passageway is the postmen's entrance; it led to the Baptist Church. At the end of the row is Chester House, with the pasageway through, where Mr Warn lived at the front of Warn's Brewery, and where my brother Eddie lived later.

From the top of Long Street we come round the corner into Church Street. Now I said that the shop on the corner of Church Street and Long Street was Mr Gething, and he took it on from Mr Clark. When I was little it was Mr Clark's shop. You have to call him Jimmy Clark because that was how he was always known. He sold toys and stuff.

The first shop in Church Street was a tobacconist. The owner was an Australian. My father used to go in there. Then there was Witchell, blacksmith and ironmonger: Witchell's yard, where Dad worked, and then Witchell's double fronted shop. The building used to be the Three Cups; Witchell's is a separate story.

Witchell's was on a different line of building from the next row. Round the other side of Witchell's, down in a bit, there was a Scotchman, Montgomery. That was a watch and clock shop. I remember once he was on a tedious job and he dropped something out of a clock. He stayed up all night until he found it.

Then there came the Post Office. Grace, Olive's daughter, she went to work in the Post Office. I've seen her there. Of course, the Post Office has moved since then, and there was a new Post Office in the Market Place and the old one became a butcher's. I think there were people living upstairs.

The Baptist Church from The Close car park. I used to go there with my friends and eat chocolate during services. There wasn't much for a boy to do in Tetbury in those days, except work.

There was a passage at the side of the Post Office that had the postmen's entrance, a side door that they used where they walked up to Church Street with the letters, and down the passage is the Baptist Church. It is very old, probably older than the parish church; Reg Cleaver's mother and father used to attend that church. You can't get down to the graveyard now from Church Street because it is part of The Close carpark, but there is a row of tombstones there to the Overbury family, beginning in 17-something, nearly all very young children. You wonder they carried on having them.

When I was first working I used to go to the Baptist Church sometimes with my friends when we got hold of a few pennies - I never had any before - and we managed to buy three or four bars of chocolate each and take them to the Baptist Church; I can't remember now why we did it, but we used to go to services and go up into the gallery and eat our chocolate there.

My sister Vera became manageress of the café in Church Street when the Australian Air Force was based in Tetbury. We thought she might marry one of the airmen, but when she was 21 she went to live in New Zealand where she married her cousin from Malmesbury, Bert Pike.

Back in Church Street, there is a shop there called Riddicks. It was a shoe shop. I suppose they sold a lot of boots and shoes because they had a lot of them hanging up outside. Next to that was a toy shop, Millards, that was run by two old ladies - there were several toy shops in Tetbury - and then a little café that belonged to Harveys. That was another grocers. When the Australians were in Tetbury in the first world war my sister Vera was in charge of the café. There was an ordinary house, somebody's home, between the café and Harvey's Stores.

Mr Harvey outside his shop in Church Street; his sons are standing in the doorway of the house (Talboys House). I used to play with the Harvey boys in the garden behind the Stores, and Olive worked in the shop when she left school. It became the International Stores.

I knew the Harveys at Harvey's Stores. They were there all my days, but then it became an International shop. My sister Olive worked up at Harvey's Stores. In the window there would be jars of Bovril with corks. The rats used to gnaw the corks and eat the Bovril out of the jars! I was at school with Arnold Harvey, and sometimes I went round to their house by the side door, to play. There is a door just past the shop that leads to the garden behind it. I particularly remember going into their garden down the back of the shop on Guy Fawkes night with the Harvey boys and we had a bonfire. We burned old boxes from the shop.

After they sold it (to International Stores) there was a manager, a Mr Miller, and Mrs Jones's daughter from Bath Road served there. There's a story about Edith and Mr Miller, and I'll tell it to you. It was during the second World War, when everything was rationed or if it wasn't, as they said, 'under the counter'. One day Edith was waiting in the shop while they were getting her order and one of Mr Miller's mates came in. He wasn't a customer - he was just visiting him. Mr Miller came out from behind the counter and said to the man: 'We've got so-and so in' - it was a drink, but I can't remember exactly what, something that was hard to get hold of then - 'would you like a bottle?'

'Oh, yes please,' the fellow said. And Mr Miller got him one.

Edith said, 'Can we have one?' She wasn't supposed to hear, but she had very sharp hearing.

'Well,' Mr Miller said, 'can you wait?' So she waited. I expect he thought she would give up and go home, but she stayed while all the other customers were served and then he let her have her bottle. She was late home from shopping. The other fellow wasn't even going to buy anything. Awful, isn't it?

The building is called Talboy's House now, but I never remember it being called that.

Next door was Milwards, the shoe shop where I worked when I was a boy at school. Once when I was there there was a swarm of bees that landed in the garden. There used to be trees at the back of the Church Street shops and the swarm landed on one of them, a great cluster, buzzing away, and a man came with a hat and a veil and a beeskep and shook the swarm off and into it and took them away. I got stung by a bee once at the Picket Harp. I wasn't doing anything and it came to me and stung me. You always knew whose bees they were because they all belonged to the postman, Harry Barnes, in Long Street. He was the only person in Tetbury who kept bees at the time. So I expect the bees that swarmed were from his hives.

Persis Lamb's shop was next. She was a photographer, usually of families and so on. She took the picture of our family. She had pictures of Tetbury on sale in the shop but I can't imagine that she went out and took them. It was probably her father who took them. He had the business before her. You wouldn't expect a woman to go out with a camera in the street in those days.

Chester House, before the arch, was next. It was where the Charlie Warns lived. It was another house that I didn't know the name of as a boy. The arch is the entrance to what used to be Warn's Brewery. Charlie Warn was the chief fireman of Tetbury, but he ran the job at the brewery; Charlie Warn was Jack Warn's brother. There were two brothers, but Jack seemed to live on the means of the business while Charlie Warn ran the business and did all that. It was a big place. There was all kinds of stuff in there, in the brewery. It's all altered into houses now, all the brewery buildings. They have houses all round. On the left there's some houses that have been converted from Warn's malthouse.

There were two lots of Warns, in two houses: Charlie Warn's was Chester House, where Eddie came to live with his wife Blodwen, known as Pat, and they had a guest house there. I never went into that house until

Eddie had it. That was the brewer's house. The curate lived there before Eddie and Pat had it; when they took the house they found his big black hat on the mantelpiece. I think the house belonged to Witchell then. It may have been Witchell's own house when they owned the brewery.

Next to the brewery entrance was a saddler called Mattick, coming round the corner. He was a saddler, but he more or less finished saddlering because trade was a bit slow. He used to do proper saddling, but then he was doing boots. Do you remember BROOM / WHEELWRIGHT / CARPENTER, in London Road? It was a big sign on the front of the house, between the downstairs and upstairs windows, and it changed from one word to the other according to where you were standing. It worked best if you were walking along. Mr Mattick married one of Broom's daughters.

Right in the corner, looking towards the town hall, just where the pavement goes in, was a little haberdashery shop, called 'the wool shop', run by two Miss Jeffcutts. The radio shop that came later came from the wool shop.

Round the corner, still on Church Street, to go on down, in that part of Church Street there was about three shops together. There was another Pegler: that was Pegler the grocer's shop. He used to sell all sorts of stuff. This Pegler was Jim Pegler's cousin. One day he was selling his goods in bags he had bought cheap - they must have overstocked - from William Jackson's bakery in Hull. I knew that, see, because one time I used to work for them.

Lucy West had the tobacconists next door. She was Darcy West's sister - he had a coal business and later ran a pub out past Knockdown - and they were Sam West's first family, when they lived at Cutwell Villa. Sam had his second family in the house next to the river on Black Horse Hill. I knew Lucy West, and I knew her mother very well, because she was in the Brethren.

Compton the hairdresser was next (he was a postman as well) and then there's a big house, and that was Jack Warn's house. The brewery used the passage there, too, in the business. But Jack Warn didn't seem to have much to do with the work. He was too busy playing golf and mixing with women.

The last little shop belonged to Granny Beard, where you turn into West

Street from Church Street. Of course it was interesting when I was a boy because Granny Beard used to sell sweets, ever so cheap. Farthings! You got some sweets on the scales. She put her hand in and put her hand out - the scales go down, like that! and another sweet! and she'd wrap em up. That's why everybody liked that! She must have been cheaper, mustn't she?

One thing she used to sell was a sort of cake, quite big, that Lewises the baker from Long Street took her. He made it once a week from stale bread, sugar and fruit like currants and bread with pastry all round it. It was Charlie Pride who used to bring it round to her. I used to go there on Fridays if I didn't go home from school for my dinner. You got a big piece, about five or six inches square, and it cost a penny. We enjoyed it, and it was all made of stale stuff!

THE OTHER SIDE OF CHURCH STREET

At the other end of Church Street, the other side, if you start behind the Town Hall, the first place after the war was a fish shop - Fishy Williams. Olive worked there at one time. They used to give her a cod's head to take home every weekend. Next door was another baker's shop, Topps, until Mr Topps retired. Mr Topps still had the old fashioned oven fired with faggots. Several young people came to Tetbury to work for Mr Topps. He had relations in New Church Street, and his people put them up.

Topps became Stanley Marks. They didn't bake there. All their stuff, including cakes, came from Bristol. There was a lot of fancy stuff but nobody wanted it.

And then there was a pub called the Boot that closed down and became a sort of showroom for Munday and Fowlers, and another pub next door, the Jolly Butchers. Then there was Miss Goodrich, a horrible teacher from the girls' school - all my sisters hated her - who had a little shop that sold tomatoes and lettuce and such things. Then there was another fish shop for a while, but it closed and Peter Payton took it over as a greengrocers. Later it became a chip shop. Mr Smith opened it with the compensation he got when he lost an arm in a threshing machine up at Nesley. His name was Harry: he was a wonderful footballer and he played in the first team for Tetbury even when he only had one arm.

Another very good player we had was Mr Wood, the boss of the workhouse in Gumstool Hill.

Further along Church Street there was a house that belonged to a man who was a cabinet maker who had an imbecile child, and then there was Tugwell's shop. Tugwell's was a ladies' shop. Donald the son was a toffee-nose.

They were next to the Eight Bells, where my brother Eddie spent a lot of his time when he wasn't in the Ormonds Head, and then a company butchers shop - not Tetbury people; they brought all the meat in from somewhere else. Raymond worked for them at one time, delivering meat to houses.

Next to that was Jim Pegler's old shop and a bakehouse that had belonged to someone called Maggs. That was before Pegler got his own place, Oxford House, in Long Street. Peglers delivered bread, first by horse and cart and then by van, in the country. There was a passage where they put the horse to feed it and put the harness on when they brought it up from the field where it lived on the Westonbirt road, down Bath Bridge way. It was a job to catch it and bring it into Tetbury. Lizzie Pegler, Gilbert's wife, always used to harness the horse. That place became Phillips's own shop.

Next door was the original Phillips the bakers - a very small bakehouse, like a garage. They only did bread, quite plain, and they had a horse and cart. Phillips's bakery delivered bread that was ordered: they charged a penny with the bread. One of Medcroft's sons worked for Phillips. There was no room at all there but one shop window and a space for the cart. When Pegler went Phillips enlarged and took over both buildings. Part of it was their house, and it was a good house. I don't think any of the Phillips family are left in the business.

The shop on the corner of Church Lane and Church Street, by the church entrance gate, was another Pegler, the cousin of Jim Pegler that I worked for and the brother of Pegler across Church Street. That's the shop we always called Cooleys, because it was Miss Cooley's shop before it was Pegler's. He always sold the Wilts and Gloster Standard once a week, and other newspapers.

CHURCH LANE AND THE GREEN

Round the corner in Church Lane from Cooleys there were two houses. Tanners lived in one. Mr Tanner was a workman who worked at the Union (the Workhouse) on Gumstool Hill. When you went there you knocked on the big solid door and Mr Tanner opened a small panel and your head was there with his. 'Now - what d'ye want?' It was a frightener - he always gave me a turn.

Mr and Mrs Tanner's son and Bill Box were the only boys who went to Grammar School in Malmesbury (there wasn't a proper secondary school in Tetbury, only private places). They went on their bicycles.

Near the church gates there was a family called Hills. Mr Hills was another baker. He had a big barrow and he pushed it round the town.

This picture of Church Lane is taken from the Green; Zoar Chapel is on the right and you can see the brewery chimney at the end of the lane.

Just past the gate in Church Lane there were the almshouses. Fred Walker's sister went to live in the almshouses after her parents died. I used to speak to her but I didn't serve her with bread. After the almshouses comes Barton Abbotts, the big house on the right as you get to The Green. The chauffeur was Mr Scurr and his son Eric was at school with me. Later he started a garage at Poulton.

On the left of Church Lane there was Mr Lamb's house. I think he had a licence to catch and kill rabbits from a person who owned the land and bring them home. Then there was the Vicarage, a very big house with a big garden, and then the Zoar chapel, and a private house with a sundial on the wall, Dial House. That was the last house in Church Lane.

On The Green there were some more houses beyond Barton Abbotts. One of them, with some steps going down, was where Mr and Mrs Lewis lived.

SILVER STREET AND FOX HILL

Mr Bristow lived just round the corner from the Green, in Silver Street. If he caught any of his family working he would wallop them. He didn't mind if they caught fish or got anything in a basket to deliver, or a little basket on your arm to sell things - you know, laces and things, to make money. But he was furious if they got a job. He thought it was a good idea if one of them took a couple of chickens and got rid of them. He was on the right lines, wasn't he?

Curly Cull was the sexton at the big church. He lived at the top of Fox Hill, and he had a car, an air-cooled Rover the same as I had later. There were only three cars that I knew in Tetbury when I was a boy. There were one or two vans, though - Mr Pegler always had a van, and I used to go in it with him or Gilbert. Later I went by myself.

Further down, on Fox Hill, was Holborow's workshop, a very busy place, where my brother in law, Fred Hills from Long Newnton, used to work. He had his nose almost cut off by the machines, and he left work there when he got a large part of one hand removed. After that he worked with Olive at her Post Office (OA Hills) at Long Newnton.

Then you go down Fox Hill to the station and towards Malmesbury.

Talking about Fox Hill, here's another story: they used to take the truck from the station, an iron truck, and of course you had the thing that you dragged it by, a handle, and you'd turn the handle and sit on the truck and you would go down the hill with all the fellows in. You would go right down to the station. Go down to the bottom of the hill and down a bit and turn left and you could go all the way down to the station. There was loads and loads of these trucks at the station because all the milk from surrounding used to come there to go away by train. They used to have to load that barrow up with milk churns and take it to the train and take the churns into the train and come back; and when it was left alone lads used to play about with it. And I expect the chap in the office would be one of the ones that would have a ride. It's funny, but it was like learning to drive: there was nothing about, no traffic.

This looks like a busy day at Tetbury Station, though it was a lot busier when there was a milk train or on cattle market days. Mr Ford was the usual engine driver.

Mr Ford who lived up on the Ciren road drove the engine and he used to give boys rides. I've had rides on the engine with him. Sir Walter Preston drove the engine in the first world war. The railway was well used, because all the milk from all around went there.

CHIPPING STREET

Going back to the middle of town, get to the top of Fawkes's shop, turn down the other way towards The Chipping, the first house in Chipping Street, there was a woman there called Miss Little. She had a window in the street, and she had a ledge on it, and her window was like you've seen a meat safe to keep things cool. It was made of metal, like a meat safe, metal with little holes in it. The men would sit on there nice and comfortable to talk and muse - until the woman got tired and she would put a pin through to get em moving.

Then it came Cull's. Jesse Cull had a dog. We used to call out 'Hello, Mr Cull, how's your dog?' Cull he was a faggot maker, meat faggots. Oh, beautiful, really. Things were good, there's no doubt about that, but then, things were good. Faggots. Everybody was after his faggots because they were so nice. It was in place of his big fat dog we used to say, you know, about his dog, you see. 'Have you cut up your dog?' I delivered bread there, and usually it was Mrs Cull who answered the door, and I dealt with her. But if ever he was at home he would say to me 'How do ee get on with the old woman these days?' He was a funny old man.

Then there was a seed shop. That is now a fish and chip shop - that used to be Murray's.

From there there is a great big place called The Institute where they hold all the dances and things. It's not necessarily a club - we used it once when we had a big church meeting - but it's a very big place and it went a good bit down the road, you see. At one time the Exclusive Brethren used the Institute as a temporary meeting room and held services there, but later they bought the old building at the foot of Bath Bridge and did it up, and that was where we went. Next we come to the weighbridge on the end, iron, out in the street. I don't know if there's one there now. Lorries came on it and got weighed with coal and you had to weigh the lorry first before you loaded it.

In those days the White Hart used to reach right down Chipping Street to the stables. People used to ride to the pub on horseback and they expected to find ostlers because the horses needed putting up.

In that day, when I was a kid, the Clancys had the theatre at the White Hart, in the big room at the front, upstairs; and you know the man that had the walking stick, waving it about - Charlie Chaplin - we used to go there and see him in a film, in the show they put on there. As a kid I would get in for fourpence, I think - it wasn't a cheap show!

Mr Clancy ran the theatre separately from the pub. The music came from a piano and a violin. Mr Clancy used to sing. I remember one of his songs - I learnt it from the show, and I have always sung it since:

> 'I used to stutter just the same as you
> But by persevering from the same I grew
> To say:
> "Brown bread - well buttered!"'

They were very clever, the Clancys, mother and son. Mainly he was a clown - telling jokes and stories. There were other little things during the show. One that I enjoyed was the advertising for local shops and so on, as magic lantern slides: there was one for one of old Mr Bristow's sons who was the chimney sweep at that time. But the main thing was always Charlie Chaplin. Oh, it was a good time. But the room stunk of beer and tobacco enough to kill you.

After the stables went there was the cinema. That's all gone now. Raymond, my brother, when he had Gale's shop, he was there when it burned down. And you go round the other side of it there. Then starting on the right hand side there was Godwin's, the father of the man down in Long Street. We're in The Chipping, not next to where the cinema was because after the cinema there was a yard belonging to a house in the front street; and you went down a yard to a pub as well, and they had a big yard. What I'm talking about isn't a passage, it's a way through - you go into the back of The Crown and through the pub and out the other side. The landlord was a pal of my dad's. The Crown, top of Gumstool Hill, by the Market Place. Next door was Godwin's.

THE CHIPPING

You can't miss the railings on both sides of the Chipping, where the road goes down the hill, but of course I can't tell you anything about them. I don't know the fellow that made them. I think it was a foundry in Gloucester or somewhere. But Dad put them up, when he was working for Witchell. The most noticeable thing my father did in Tetbury was the railings on both sides of The Chipping, where the road goes down the hill. He didn't cast the posts, but he put everything together. They are in a bad way now at the top, broken and patched up.

Dad built these railings in The Chipping. I always say it's like having a monument.

It's like having a monument in a way, isn't it? As well as the railings in The Chipping he did the iron railings at Highgrove, too. And he put the irons in the coping of the Wiltshire Bridge, where it used to say GLOUCESTERSHIRE one way and WILTSHIRE the other. The boundary isn't there any more. Do you know where Wiltshire is now? It's nearer Malmesbury, it's further up the road, at Fred Hills Auntie's, a farm called Merchants Farm.

At the other side of the Chipping there was what they call the Malthouse. I'm talking about the top of the Chipping Steps. I don't know anything about the Malthouse, but that's where they used to work. They used to have about three times in a bag, to be made into malt, than a man could carry. The maternity nurse used to live next door, the lady that came with a black bag and a baby, and then Mr and Mrs Elsey. He was the boss for Pellys, The Priory, and I used to work for him when I worked at the Priory. He looked after the house, the whole job, and he was the gardener, too. They had a cowman who looked after their cows and did other jobs around the house, a man who looked after the horses - they had hunters - an assistant gardener, and me, as well as house servants.

Wiltshire Bridge over the River Avon used to be on the boundary of Gloucestershire. If you walk on the bridge and look carefully you can still see some of the iron bars set in lead that Dad put in where the coping was breaking away. The picture was taken from the Station Approach.

On that level of Chipping Steps where you were standing, you looked across towards The Priory. You'd be up very high, and you could see where we worked in the garden up there. You could see the garden had got a greenhouse in it, right upon the top. The greenhouse was full of beautiful, beautiful black grapes, and - there's the garden, and there's the wall there - now in a little space like that there was the back door of the lad that worked there, the fellow I was working with - his name was Bill Maisey. He used to drop his mother down a bunch of grapes on a string. He used to slide up the window - professionally cut the bunch of grapes - put it on a string - and the gardener never found out.

And the point was, there was a fig tree with only one fig on it. It wasn't in the greenhouse, it was in the garden. I only just nicely had my eye on it. I waited and waited and waited until one day I was tempted to take it. The next day or two afterwards the boss himself came looking for his fig and I said I should have thought the birds would have had it. I said

'Reckon that the birds would have had that, don't you?' No, I'd had that! I waited for it to get somewhere near ready. And ate it. I could keep on like that for ever, I suppose.

I went to work for the Pellys at The Priory after I gave up working for Pegler the first time. It was interesting but they didn't pay me much.

I left my mark on The Priory when I worked there. The lawn is made from grass that I had weeded out when I was helping the gardener.

When I was working at The Priory a man came round from next door: 'Have you seen our pigeon? I just killed it and it flew away!'

You could say I left my mark on The Priory. The head gardener, the boss of everything, was going to make a lawn. My job was to go along the ash path (they used to make garden paths from the ashes and cinders from the coal fires) with a wheelbarrow and pick out any blades of grass that were growing there - carefully! Then I had to take the barrow back to the gardener and he planted the grass in a big area that he had prepared. The lawn that we made is still there, by the terrace.

If you look up, you see there is a kind of stone railing round the top of the house. Up there I found a big stone, and I wedged it in between two of the posts. I wonder if it's still there?

CHIPPING STEPS

I slipped and fell near the bottom of Chipping Steps when I was selling cabbages door to door. I hit my chin on the step and got scarred for life.

I can tell you about Chipping Steps. If you could see my chin you would know about this because I've still got the mark. I was selling cabbages from Kew Gardens, the allotments in Herd Lane. I used to sell a lot of the cabbages door to door for threepence apiece. I had a truck to carry them on, beautiful big cabbages, and pulled them round Tetbury.

Well, one day I parked my truck at Chipping Steps where it gets to the bottom of the Chipping, the first flight there, and started to walk down carrying a couple of cabbages, and the next thing I knew was that the woman from the first house had brought me out a chair and got me in it. Then there were crowds of people around. The rest of the folk in Chipping Steps had come out to watch the pantomime. I had fallen and knocked myself right out and cut my chin. It was a big bang. I don't remember any bleeding, or at least there wasn't much blood, but I was certainly knocked out. I don't suppose there's much blood in your chin!

When I had recovered a bit I went on selling the cabbages.

When Edith first came to Tetbury I showed her where I got the mark on my chin and she took a picture of the steps. It's a champion one. When I look at the picture I always think of what happened to me that day.

There was a man who lived by Chipping Steps, where I fell down. He used to get into fights. He used to say 'He who fights and runs away lives to fight another day!'

At the bottom of the road where you go up the Chipping from Cirencester Road there was always a sign that said PLEASE SLACKEN AIM REIN WHEN GOING UPHILL. I don't know whether it's still there.

I used to go down the Chipping with a barrow to the coal merchant at the station and get half a hundredweight of coal for the fire at home. Everyone did that.

Then there was a coal man as well, who went round with a horse and a wagon. His name was Charlie Hills, a blind man, and he used to shout as he came along the road 'Charlie on the roller! Cuckoo!' His horse knew the way and stopped for him and would go to the next place where he had to stop. 'Coo-al! Coo-al!' and the horse would stop. The horse seemed to do what it wanted to, but it wouldn't go on when it was supposed to be stopped. Charlie always managed the change correctly.

GUMSTOOL HILL

Tetbury was small enough in those days that you knew everyone's business. There was a policeman one time whose wife was my father's cousin (maybe through my grandfather's second wife, in Malmesbury); now, the policeman used to spend the night with a widow, a lady who lived in a house behind the workhouse. Her husband who died used to work at Upton House where he was the chauffeur. Nobody knew about the affair, of course; I don't think Dad knew.

There used to be lots and lots of tramps. They paid to get in a place at Malmesbury and then they would go on to Tetbury and Stroud. If they had no money when they reached Tetbury they would go to the Union Workhouse at the top of Gumstool Hill. The Union would give them some work and a bed for the night. If they had some money they would go to the dosshouse in West Street. They used to sleep on a rope. If you gave a tramp anything he would make a mark for the others.

Tramps stayed at Tetbury Union. When it stopped being the Workhouse it became the Maternity Hospital. Edith had Elizabeth Ann there; my cousin Lily from Crossroads at Shipton Moyne was the hospital cook.

But when I was a boy the main thing was the Casual Ward at the Workhouse. Tramps would go there and get a bed for the night. Every man who stayed there had to do some work in the morning and they gave him breakfast.

Then the workhouse was made into a maternity hospital, and of course Elizabeth Ann was born there, and Mr Herbert's grandchild at about the same time, and a lot of other children too.

There's a story about that. On October the second, 1945, I was delivering bread there - they had loads of bread, no end of it - when I was going round Tetbury with the van. I asked there, and they said 'You've got a daughter!' and I said - silly, wasn't I? - 'You can have anything you want!'

What we would call a mental hospital now we used to call the Asylum. In Tetbury it was called Hill House, and it was just a bit down Gumstool Hill after the workhouse, but a bit hidden. The people, the inmates, would go for walks through Tetbury, right up Upton Road and out into the country. When I was a little boy at home I could see them coming up the road past our house, running and skipping, some of them, and doing funny things. They wouldn't hurt anyone, though some people were frightened of them. The boss keeper, the man who controlled Hill House, Mr Day, you could talk to him, but he twitched all the time and when he walked he sometimes trotted. He would go run and stop and then run on. You could have mistaken him for an inmate!

My father was always being called to the asylum to do jobs, and it was often the same one: they had iron bars over the fires to stop the people falling in, and the inmates used to tear them off. Dad had the job of replacing them. But he did other things there. Once I went to help him to do a job there, and I remember being up above the big room with the fireplace, looking down on the people through a trapdoor. I had to do something like that once myself, when I swept the chimneys there.

Right at the bottom of the hill there is the cattle market. If you came down to the cattle yard and went on you came to the rifle range. When I was working at Kew Gardens I used to go across a little bridge to the rifle range at the bottom of the gardens. If you came down to the cattle yard and turned sharp left you came to the pond, and if you turned sharp right you got to the rifle range. Or I used to go down the Chipping, past the railings, you know, and down into the Market Place. In the bottom the river ran into the pool and out again, near the bottom of Gumstool Hill. You walked along the river and over it to the rifle range. I used to go to the rifle range to shoot the rifles when I was quite young. I can't remember anyone else that went; they were mostly young, and the people I remember best were old people and those about the same age as Mother and Dad.

It was in a place before the river goes under the bridge. It was for teaching you to shoot, a local thing, not the army. It started before I took over Kew Gardens.

There was nothing there but practising, me and other young men. You had to pay a bit, for the ammunition, but it was only pennies. That was a good job, because nobody of us ever had more than twopence. But if I did have a few pennies in that day that is what I spent it on.

MARKET PLACE

Webbs was the department store in the Market Place. Some parts of their shop were across the road.

Raymond and Elizabeth Ann are talking to me near the Macfisheries. We were all together in the Market Place that day. Cliff, Elizabeth Ann's husband, took the picture.

If you go back up to the Market Place, the next place to the fish shop, going towards Silver Street, was Webb's, a very important shop. It was an outfitters for ladies and gentlemen and drapers and milliners among other things. When Mr and Mrs Webb died they were both buried in the little graveyard at the bottom of Bath Bridge. Next to Webb's was a big house and then a goodie shop - they only sold sweets - and next to that a fish and chip shop. Then at the end of the road there was Taylor's, right on the corner. He was a cousin of my mother's. She told me about him but we didn't know them really. They sold sweets, tobacco and lots of other things. He was into everything in Tetbury. One of his things was to get the fire engine going when it was needed.

Opposite Taylors was the Talbot Hotel where Rene was a barmaid after she came home from Chedworth. I remember the landlord because he had to do with the church choir, and when choirboys went into the pub he always acknowledged them.

Then there was a big house where Mr and Mrs Weare lived, Crewe House, next to the Talbot. His daughter, Miss Weare, carried on living there after Mr and Mrs Weare moved somewhere else. Mr Weare had a cold bath every day. He was a very old man when I knew him.

There are two cars and no parking restrictions in the Market Place. My sister Rene was a barmaid at The Talbot; Holborow's, the builder's, who did everything in Tetbury, is on the left.

Next to that was Hussey's the plumbers and then Mr and Mrs Fry's house. By this time you were in Union Street. There was a passage through their house that led up some steps to another house at the back which was the Exclusive Brethren's old church before they bought the chapel at the bottom of Bath Bridge. People came there from Malmesbury as well as Tetbury. You walked down the passage and out through the yard and there was a big pipe there to catch the water, and you walked past. The chapel was like a house but you had to go up some steps to it. There were some people that kept chickens underneath, and there were fleas. The first time I went there with Edith she got them. It had electricity very early, when houses first had electric lighting in Tetbury. When the Brethren got the building for their church Mr Pockett wired it for electricity. It was like magic! That building was very old and strongly built, and he couldn't put the wires inside the wall of the church, but he laid the strands neatly on the surface.

Then of course there was the Tetbury Union workhouse. But by that time you were in Gumstool Hill.

Across the road there is the Crown Inn, and on the corner of the street coming back from Gumstool Hill there was a young man who had a business of photography. I think his name was Harding, but no relation to the people at Upton. Then there was Ives' Transport, and I think that used to be a pub, and a petrol station, and then another shop belonging to the Webbs that was a carpet shop, and a tailor who worked for them as well. Clarence worked for the jeweller's next door, Satteley's, and trained there as a watch maker after he gave up his job with the solicitor. The White Hart Hotel came next, on the corner of Chipping Street.

CIRENCESTER ROAD

Gumstool Hill from The Royal Oak, Cirencester Road. There is a horse-drawn Great Western Railway van on its way to the station.

Jones at the Oak was a haulier with a steam engine. They did furniture removals. Immediately behind the Oak was Kew Gardens, where our allotment was. All down there are gardens now, but in those days it used to be the scavenge heap, and it was always burning. The gardens were made of rubbish from the scavenging. They burned it all. I had my allotment at Kew Gardens, the first garden at the top of Herd Lane. Dad was the tenant first and then I took it on. That was where I grew the cabbages that I used to take round Tetbury to sell. I grew everything there. The potatoes always had scab, but they were quite good to eat.

NEW CHURCH STREET

In New Church Street there was Mrs Holland and her sons on one corner and Mr Macdonald from the garage at the other. Then there was Mellish the doctor, and Mr Houghton next door was his chauffeur.

Next door was where the blind coalman lived.

Mr Ruddle was a cobbler. He used to live in the next house to the Blue Bell pub in New Church Street, towards the school. Oh, he was a funny man. He was funny in the head, I think. He was a cobbler, like the man in Long Street, but he only used to mend old shoes.

There was a big garden belonging to a Mr Crew, the man who went round the schools and picked up the register to see if we were really there in the class. He would call all our names: 'Frank Peters!'

'Yes, sir!'

He wasn't the truant catcher; I think he was one of the school governors.

There was a man called Charlie Barrett (there was more than one Charlie Barrett in Tetbury then) who lived in the next house. And then there was another chauffeur, and his wife who had a dog. It used to lick her all over. And it would go and lick the bottom of telegraph poles, too. I think that was what killed her. Then there was a house with railings, and a milkman lived there, but he didn't stay, and a man from Harvey's Stores in Church Street went there - he was the new boss of the Stores - and his wife; but she had no idea how to look after him. One day, soon after they moved in, he came home for his meal and found her crying. She wanted to boil some eggs and she didn't know how.

The next house was Miss Heath, the Head of the girls' school, and then Jackie Dance, the Head Master. Then there is the cemetery, St Saviour's churchyard. The church is closed now. I don't know what they will do with it. Isn't it peculiar? They built that church for what they called the 'poor people' - people who couldn't afford to pay the rent of a pew in the big church. Fancy expecting people to pay rent for their seats in church! It's really strange, isn't it? Fancy charging people to go to church!

There used to be wooden tombstones in the New Church Street cemetery. Do you know, I knew everybody that was buried there with a wooden tombstone. All our people are in the churchyard there, you know.

There was some work going on at the church one time, and they had scaffolding up, and they were taking their time over the work. Mr Hedges had something to do with it: he got fed up with the slowness of the work and he went up the scaffold himself and did it straight away.

After the churchyard there was Charlie Crew, who was one of my mates. We used to go gleaning with them. Lucy Crew was his sister.

The next house, up by the Knap there, was Harry Smith. He was the father of all the Smiths in Tetbury. He had a brother, and between them they used to do all the whitewashing and plastering that was to be done in the town.

Another Charlie Barrett's grandmother lived next door; then there was Frank Walker, the brother of Fred. They were partners in the haulage business that they ran from Fred's house in Upton Road. They used to haul stuff from the gasworks at one time. All the waste sulphur was taken by the Walkers in their cart.

Then it was opposite the school, and called Charlton Road, and another family of Hortons, the Gilbert Hortons (there were at least three families of Hortons). Their son was Hubert Horton who drove his father's goat-cart. He was a baker, like me, but for Phillips.

The National School faced on to the Knap, with the wall of The Close at one side with big beech trees. We used to collect the beech mast when it fell from the trees and eat it.

Mr Box, Bill Box's father, lived just opposite the school. He used to be a building fellow. He worked for Chavenage House and he did a lot with racing pigeons and he always won. Bill Box was at school with me. Bill went to the Grammar School in Malmesbury later because there wasn't one in Tetbury then. He went because he was a clever boy. He went together with young Tanner, who lived at the second house in Church Lane, by the Green. Bill had sisters - one of them married a man from Shipton Moyne.

COOMBERS MEAD AND GASHOUSE ROW

You've heard people speak of Coombers Mead? Now it's the first part of London Road, but it used to be both sides of the crossing, including the first part of New Church Street; people usually mean London Road when they say Coombers Mead, but I call that part Gas House Row, before the gasworks, where Eddie and Pat used to live, before they moved to Church Street, and they used to call all of London Road Back Lane. Mrs Daily Mail used to live in one of the houses in Gas House Row. She was Mrs Jim Smith, and you could see her any time standing at the door of her house shouting out the news to anyone who would listen.

There was a woman who lived in the first house but she came from Mount Pleasant. She was a cobbler's wife. When Clarence was a baby she was looking after him and she let him fall into the fire and burn himself.

Aunt Alice lived in Gashouse Row before she was married to my uncle Albert, the coastguard. She was Miss Phillips before she was Mrs Vizor. Mr Ewlands lived in that house after that. Auntie Alice's house was two or three doors down from Gearing's shop on the corner.

Mr Gearing was very good. It was a little shop and in that day nothing was wrapped up and packed like it is now. He didn't have any machinery in his shop; he sold bacon off the piece without a bacon machine: he cut it into rashers with a knife and put each piece on the scales. If a lady came in for a pound of bacon he would get his knife and a sharpener and start singing while he sharpened the knife: 'Umm.. aahh...aahh...' and then he would get a piece of paper and lay it on the scales and wipe his nose and then he would gently cut a rasher and place it on the paper, still singing, and wipe his nose with his hand, and smooth the bacon out, 'Mmm...aahh...aahh...mmm...aahh.' Then he would gently cut another one or two rashers and wipe his nose with his fingers, and use them to spread the bacon out smooth on the paper, and then wipe his nose again. He was a dirty man. People used to stand there in the shop while he wiped his nose and did the rashers. I used to 'do' Mr Gearing for Edith - you know, pretend to be him cutting her a pound of rashers - she always seemed to enjoy it!

Mr Vick was the butcher across London Road, on the same side as the Plough. He used to get the sheep to follow him. He would say, 'Come on! Come on!' and they would trot up behind. That was when he was taking them to kill them. Mr Vick was Eric Vick's father. Mr Vick was in the

Open Brethren, but Eric had nothing to do with it. He would take his father out, but he wouldn't go into the church.

When I was quite small Mr Vick had his shop next to Pride's milk shop and Pride's Dairy in London Road. Mr Vick had goats that he milked. He kept them in Blind Lane and he used to go to and fro with them.

Mr Vick had notices in his shop asking people to come to the services. And his wife used to try to make me do the right thing.

When I was knocking around, and hadn't got a job, I used to go and help Vick to kill the pigs. Just yuck them up on a board and stick them. Cut the throat and drain the blood out (they probably sold it to go to the hospitals!). No, they actually use it for black pudding!

When I helped Mr Vick kill the pigs he would give me a pound of sausages - the very, very best. That was when I was a boy, before I started at Pegler's full time.

Mr Vick had a wagonette to hire out. My mother used to hire the wagonette off Mr Vick.

There were three Vick children: there were Eric and his sister Gladys who had their own butchery business at Northfield and then they took over the London Road shop and ran it together afterwards. They were rowing all the time. And there was another child, a son who was ill all the time, lying down.

WEST STREET

I knew any amount of people in West Street, but I can't remember them all now.

One of them was called Cuckoo Walker. He used to walk every day to the farm up Blind Lane, Warner's. They called him Cuckoo Walker because he couldn't say it - he couldn't say 'cuckoo'. When they heard the cuckoo, people would say, 'What's that bird, Mr Walker?' and he would say 'It's a oo-oo.' He said 'oo-oo'. So they used to call him 'Mr Oo-oo'. He was one of Mother's relatives. Years after I had left Tetbury, when I was back for the funeral, I met a man who was digging the grave for Billy Lewis, my sister Rene's husband. I asked him, 'Are you Mr Walker's son from West Street?'

'Yes,' he said.

'Well, do you mind if I ask you, did he have a speech impediment?'

'What do you mean, a speech impediment?' he said. So I showed him.

'Oh, yes,' he said, 'that was my Dad.'

There is not much of this view left nowadays. It shows Harper Street, now West Street. They changed the name because Harper Street had a bad reputation. I went to school this way every morning from Milwards shoe shop in Church Street, while the School Master was ringing the bell.

Of course that's the old part of Tetbury, and it wasn't really West Street then. It used to be called Harper Street. They changed the name to West Street because the girls going out to service couldn't get a place because they came from Harper Street. In the early days West Street was all fighting. Mr Pulley, who kept the Drum and Monkey - that isn't the proper name, it's the Prince of Wales - they were common people that ran it, a bit rough, but it was what was needed. He had a whole gang of sons.

I knew a lot more people in West Street. Mrs Spencer, that lived practically next door to the Drum and Monkey - Mrs Spencer - you know her? She only used to do that bit of her hair on her forehead, just there. You never saw her without her hat, pulled down. She never washed. She used to stand at her door, leaning on her elbow. I went to sweep her chimney when I had the sweeping business, but you couldn't see the fireplace for the ashes!

When Edith was ill and sweating she said to the doctor, 'If Mrs Spencer sweated like this, she'd be buried in the muck!' In her early days Mrs Spencer was an orphan girl and she was put out from a house to work for Mrs Cox at the top of Bath Bridge. Mr Cox was the rat-catcher. Then she married this fellow Spencer - I wonder how. He was odd as well.

You know what he was, a cowman. For Pride's Dairy, London Road, where Mrs Pride made good ice cream. How they came to employ him I don't know, though he wasn't as dirty as she was. She was awful. That's only a yarn that she used to sunbathe naked in her back garden. Now who could have seen her in her back garden? You would have to climb over what's at the back of her garden, a big wall: The Close. The Close wall runs right round there, you know. And right round by the School, and right up the road.

A man called Hodges had a shop at the school end of West Street. That was where the kids used to go for sweets.

There was a lot of Cleavers, mostly brothers I should say. I remember Esther Cleaver. She lived up there in West Street too. When I took Edith home to Tetbury first of all we met her. She was a rough woman but very nice - Esther the Queen, it's in the Bible - she was delighted to see me. She was delighted because I always got on well with people. When I was with Edith and we were walking up Church Street she shouted out 'Oh, hello, Frankie!'

Esther Cleaver was an old woman She had a son, Teddy, who was decent. My friend Reg Cleaver lived opposite, in West Street, down an alleyway and round to the right, facing the other way out.

You know, a lot of the houses in West Street are built on a hill: you go through the front door and through the house and you are going down the hill. One lot of Cleavers lived in one of those houses, and at the back, that is, down the hill, they had a fish and chip shop. I was there one day delivering their bread. They weren't paying any attention to me, and while I was putting two loaves down on the table I overheard two women talking. One of them said to the other, 'No, we're all right.' I listened while I was standing there with the bread. She went on 'I go where I like and my husband goes where he likes!' I knew what she meant because I knew about her. She meant she was looking after a fella and her husband was looking after another woman. I knew who all of them were.

I did know her husband: he got a job after this with the Post Office, and while he was there he thought he had information early about the pools results and he did something to claim he had won. He had an idea that he would get away with it but he got caught and he was sent to prison in Gloucester.

Their son, if they were having a rabbit, he would eat every bit of bone. He could do anything with a pen, handwriting and drawing, but he could do nothing else. He married a girl who was a servant for Major Little and Lady Guendolene at Upton House, when Mrs Medcroft used to work for them as what they called 'the odd woman'.

Sharpes were another West Street family. One of them, Maurice Sharpe, lived part way down Cutwell Hill.

There were always Woods in West Street, a rough lot. But there was one that got away and married Mrs Woodley, and it was their daughter that married Philip Herbert from Down Ampney.

There was a man called White who kept the dosshouse halfway along West Street, or probably Harper Street at that time. It was for tramps. They used to go cadging to pay for it. It was quite a trade. Alec White was this White's son and he worked at Wrights as a printer with Mr Price from Upton Road. He was a comical fellow. He used to call us two boys who worked there Simon Peter and Jacob Jones. It was Jacob's real name. Alec was a nice fellow. I would be going to school with his younger brother.

There was another White that lived for a while in the cave at Hermit's Wood. He came from Shipton Moyne originally.

Now old Mr Pegler's wife had a sister called Mrs Cox who lived in West Street. She was a cockeyed woman! Mrs Pegler thought I didn't know who she was, that she was her sister, but of course I did. Mrs Pegler would say to me 'You tell that Mrs Cox we must have some money!' because they ran up a bill at the shop. Mrs Pegler said 'We can't afford to keep people!' pretending that she didn't know who Mrs Cox was.

I went to Mrs Cox and asked for the money, but she never paid what she owed. She said 'Go and find Mr Cox and tell him!' Then she would start to get some weeny potatoes together and scrabble something for his dinner while I went to get paid. He was a brutish man and he used to lounge about under the Town Hall. He was one of a number of men who were out of work, and they used to loaf there, walking up and down to keep warm. He killed a fellow once when there was a show on in Tetbury. He got drunk and hit the man and he died. Mr Cox would have a drink from time to time and then have a go at somebody, and I think that's what happened this time. I think the magistrates at Gloucester were more interested in the show than they were in him and that's how he got off.

I never got any money from him.

I knew loads of other people in West Street. One was my friend Eric Wilkins, the butcher's nephew. He was another of the Open Brethren.

There were three girls called Cox in Tetbury, in Cottons Lane, that never got married. I don't know exactly where in Cottons Lane they lived. You went through an alley-way and there was a row of houses, you see, but I didn't go in there. The father was a road sweeper. None the more, he was a decent man. He was a bit of a cripple, but a nice man. I knew them because I didn't know anybody but I knew everybody! I just know them. Anyrate, what I was surprised with, and you mightn't believe it, they were real spick and span girls and they helped the mother. They laundered. They stayed at home and laundered. In and out. And I thought they would never get married.

I used to think, What lovely girls! Like that, and nobody seems to be interested. They must have been decent girls. They were a bit older than me but they didn't get married. This is always how I checked up: I thought to myself, I wasn't interested in girls at all myself, but I often thought, Why didn't they ever get married? When they got older they all married, when men had more sense. It's true, that. They were eligible girls when they got married, but they were older. Nobody hung on to them, if you know what I mean. It only proved, in my estimation, that they were decent girls. They may not have been playgirls.

One of them married a man from Northfield. They called him Slogger Townsend and they lived quite happy. I noticed them when they were married. They were well dressed and everything. Looked after. I suppose they didn't get out to work, for one thing.

I was what they call a 'good boy' because I wasn't usually in trouble - I was always working! But several boys I knew used to be destructive. They used to go down and smash windows - just like that. The police were always running after boys.

There were usually three policemen for the whole Tetbury area, one sergeant and two constables. Often there was nothing for them to do, but when I was quite young there were some events like one of these prison riots you hear about. There has been nothing like it since, as far as I know.

What happened was that the West Street boys, for the chief part, the clever ones, were going to work with sticks and things after the boys from the other part of Tetbury, and causing a bother. They pretended to be mad, and they all had nicknames. I'm sorry, I can't remember what they were now! But they were chiefly from West Street, which was a bit rough then, and they ran after people who came from the other side. The policeman on duty was always running after them.

One of the policemen was a big man and he carried a big stick, a walking stick, as well as his truncheon, and if he caught boys doing something they shouldn't - WHACK! He would hit them with his big stick. And it was a big thing, calling out to him and getting him to run after them. It was tantalising him, you see. They did other things, too.

Once these boys got into the Town Hall, which they would do if they got a chance; they got up there and opened all the windows. The police came up after them and shut the windows but they couldn't find the boys, and they came out again. I'm sure I don't know where the boys got hided, but they did, and they came and opened the windows again. The police were down in the road and threatened them with fire and pestilence, but they didn't catch them.

The boys weren't wicked. They were just 'having some fun' with the police.

BATH ROAD

If you cross over West Street, going towards the bridge, it's Bath Road, and the first place was the blacksmith's, and then there was a man called Mr Goulding. There were only two more houses: one had children from the orphanage, and the last one belonged to Cox the rat-catcher. There was a saying about the rat-catcher: 'He always does his Best'. But I don't want to say anything about Mrs Best. He had two nicknames: 'Mousey' (because of his job) and 'Sligo' which was a name he got from school for being more eager to do things than most: if the teacher said 'Is there anybody who can go...?' (because the teachers always wanted boys to run errands for them) he would call out 'S'll I go, Sir?' So we called him Sligo. Sligo Cox.

The building to the right of the bridge is a house now, but I first remember it when it was where Warn's Brewery vehicles were kept. Then it became the Meeting Room for The Brethren.

The little building at the bottom of Bath Bridge on the right, that was a garage for Warns the brewers. When it was closed it was cast into a church for the Exclusive Brethren by Alf Davis.

During the war we lived at number 6, at the bottom of the bridge.

The Meeting room at the bottom of Bath bridge, from our house. I went there three times every Sunday and at least twice in the evening during the week, unless I was tired out. This picture would be taken in the War.

Mr Brown, Charlie Brown the farmer, lived at the funny looking house, the toll house at the top of Bath Road. You know he had a dairy there, and did everything with cold water. Nothing was sterilized when they were separating milk, and when he was inspected there was all sorts of stuff growing in the handles of things. My dad knew about it because he was always mending stuff for them. Dad had to do all the repairs for things that got broken on the farm.

Charlie Brown had fields with his family both sides of Tetbury. There was a scene you ought to know about from the first world war involving Mr Brown. You know, in that war there were Scouts as well as Volunteers, and they weren't Boy Scouts but grown men, and these men were training with rifles in one of Charlie Brown's fields, the one opposite our house in Upton Road. They were guarding the water tower up at the Waterworks. Charlie Brown walked up there one day and he was challenged, and didn't give the answer. They knew who he was, but when he walked up to them they challenged him and when he wouldn't answer them, they shot him in the leg! You've got to answer when they call 'Who goes there?' because it's the Crown that demands it, but Charlie Brown didn't answer and got shot!

A few years ago I went to see Mrs Jones, Ada Jones, when she was living at The Priory. She used to live opposite us in Bath Road with her husband Bert and the family. We lived at number 6 - they call it The Old Toll House now - I don't know why. I don't think it was ever a toll house. The one at the top of the hill is still there.

Mr Jones used to drive a horse and come home for his dinner and tie the horse up to the fence by our house with a nosebag on. They sold us a boy's bicycle for John once.

The next house down Black Horse Hill from us used to be a bakehouse. I don't remember it as a bakehouse, but I saw the sign in print on the wall when they renovated the building. Black Horse Hill was the roadway, you know, before Bath Bridge was built. They had a trace horse or two on hand for anyone who would be wanting to drive up. Mr Sam West lived in the house. He was a quarrelsome man, too, a hot-tempered fellow. He would think nothing of taking his belt off to a child. His proper wife, his first wife, was Exclusive Brethren. After she died, when he was an old man, he picked up a girl, a servant working at one of the big houses at The Chipping. She came from West Street. There was a daughter.

Between our house and West's house there was a churchyard. It belonged to the Exclusive people. I don't think there was another one anywhere. That's where Gilbert Pegler and his wife are buried. He was only in his sixties when he died. His father, Jim Pegler, used to look after it and cut the grass and look after the trees and bushes. Some of my Auntie Alice's relations, the Wilkinses from Coombers Mead, went to the Exclusive meeting. There were plenty of Wilkinses, though they didn't all go to the Exclusives' meeting. Some were at the Open Brethren meeting. One was Eric Wilkins who was my friend.

All the Barretts were buried there, too. Another family that went to the Brethren's Meeting was the Webbs who had the big shop where the new Post Office is - the drapers and ladies' outfitters. Worthy Kidd's granddaughter worked there. She married a policeman.

It is marvellous how you know people. You know all about them.

HAMPTON STREET

It used to run from Coombers Mead to the corner of Chavenage Lane. Then it was called Upton Road, from the high wall at the corner. The main things in Hampton Street were Cook's Brewery and the combing house for wool. All Tetbury was a hive of industry, but particularly the combing house. That was busy up to the end of the first World War, for uniforms, but then it stopped. The big garage that belonged to Pikes was there, and the Register Office, and The Grey House where the Gipps lived; and there was the Greyhound where my dad used to go when he had finished in the evening.

The two breweries, Warns and Cooks, had beautiful wells. The breweries were there because of the water, choice water, wherever it came from, to suit the job. Warns, you know, was in Church Street, and Cooks was in Hampton Street. All the deliveries were done by horses and carts. Say Mr Cleaver, who worked for Warns, had to go to Malmesbury, he could only do one journey, loading and unloading.

When Cooks stopped being a brewery somebody bought it and turned it into a washing mill, a laundry, and they called it the TETBURY HAND AND STEAM LAUNDRY. Then Fred Hills' relations from the farm took it on. You used to be able to see into the laundry from Hampton Street, see all the machinery of the laundry.

Joe Roseblade was one who worked for Cook's Brewery. He lived in the toll house in Hampton Street. Joe used to grow marrows and enter them in Tetbury Show. He grew them very big. Once some of us leaned over the wall and carved his name on his biggest marrow when they were all quite small, and we watched it as it grew. The name grew with the marrow, and of course the marrow grew bigger than all the others. He wanted to put it in the show, but he couldn't, because it had his name on it!

– THE THIRD PART –

Living at Upton Road

*O*ur house was number 3 Upton Road. The house is still there but the number is 78 Hampton Street. There used to be fields from Chavenage Lane and then our row of houses. Upton Road was a sort of hamlet all by itself. The house has a porch, a front room, a back room that held the sink and a boiler for the clothes, and a pantry down stairs (we kept a barrel of cider there, and my dad's rifle); there was a winding flight of stairs - when Mother died they had to bring her coffin down on end - and upstairs there was one bedroom for Mother and Dad and a landing for the rest of us. Mother had a harmonium in the bedroom and there was a piano in the living room.

There were four houses in a row, beautiful stone built houses, built by Westonbirt House: Bert Slade, the Boultons, us and the Medcrofts (all the Medcrofts used to live at number 4 - I don't know how they all fitted in). The Medcrofts left and the Hortons moved in.

Highgrove Lodge, Doughton, was where Mother and Dad lived when they were first married and their first baby, Mabel, was born here. Mother had the job of opening the gate when the carriage came through.

Mother and Dad had nine children altogether: Mabel was born, and died when she was very little, when they lived at the lodge at Highgrove where Mother was gatekeeper; the rest of us were all born at Upton Road: Vera, Olive, Irene, me, Eddie, Laura, Raymond and Clarence.

I was the fourth child to survive. I was the first boy. I think they must have been very pleased that I was a boy, you know, there must have been excitement, because you know what they did? They planted an apple tree in the garden when I was born. The tree had beautiful apples. It was called a Beauty of Bath - a very good apple, a summer apple. It was a real beauty of Bath, but it didn't last that long, and after it died my father grew a plum tree in the same spot. But the apples were beautiful. As far as I know they didn't do anything for any of the other children.

A person I delivered bread to when I was a baker was Bert Slade, who lived in the first of the four houses in our row. He liked his bread burned black. I kept it in the oven all day for him. You weren't supposed to sell it like that, but that was how he wanted it - like charcoal. I had to get it to him without anyone knowing. As children we would hear 'Bert' from Mother and Dad, though he was no relation, and we would repeat it; but we would get stepped on for that and told to say 'Mister Slade'. After Bert Slade died Mrs Purnell from the Plough at the corner of Long Street bought the house.

Mrs Boulton lived next door, at 2 Upton Road. She wasn't a very pleasant woman to have as a neighbour. She was what you might call harsh in her manner. We didn't have much to do with her as a matter of fact. It was quite different with her lad, Reg Boulton: he was always nice and friendly. He was quite a lot older than me. Mrs Boulton wasn't his mother. He was Mrs Boulton's daughter's son.

Mother was cleaning the grate one day and Reg came after me, from their house. He had put a mask on, a children's mask, and I was frightened to death. I remember running indoors and getting a tall chair and pushing it up to the fireplace. I knew Mother was cleaning the grate, and I came to be shielded by my Mother!

Mr and Mrs Medcroft lived next door to us, at number 4, before the Hortons. She was a hard working woman. She came from Oaksey in Wiltshire. Their children were young then. There were so many Medcrofts that all lived there at the same time. I don't know how many. There were at least eight children living there - many, many children.

They went to live in Chavenage Lane, but a lot of them were born at Upton Road. One of them went to work for Peter Scott at Slimbridge. There was Bill, and Charles, Little Shit (that was Fred - they always called him Little Shit), and Goggy. There was Ours'n - that was Mr Medcroft. Mrs Medcroft never called him anything but Ours'n. He was a shepherd and at one time he earned eight and six a week to keep I don't know how many of them. He got a shilling beer money for taking the sheep and lambs to market, and he used to save it.

Fred Medcroft was working for a time at The Priory stables in London Road; I used to go and help him get water and things like that when I had nothing better to do. At another time Fred was a caretaker and gamekeeper at Ledgemore, beyond Chavenage Green. He was always there with the birds to protect them. Another time he worked at the depot next to Wisteria in Upton Road.

Goggy was friends with Bill Cox, whose dad was Major Cosmo Little's chauffeur at Upton House. They were really bosom friends, but about once a year they had a terrible fight in the field across from our house. Then they were friends again for another year.

Nelly, the daughter, went to Australia years ago, when she was only a kid.

The Medcrofts used to stand their frying pan up against the wall so that Nigger, the big dog at Wisteria, the last house, would come into their house, and she would let him lick the pan clean. Then they could use it again!

Mr and Mrs Price lived next door to Medcroft's in Upton Road. Mr Price worked for Wright's the printers. I got on with him all right. Mr Price had a brother called Alec who went to be a sailor. He was quite a bit older than me. After he had been in the navy for some time he just didn't come back.

The Price's son was called Cecil. He was one I was at school with. I remember he couldn't eat peas! He was in the church choir with me and we went on an outing and we had dinner - it was a party - and there were peas. He couldn't eat them. Later on he played in the Tetbury band and did very well.

I remember the grandfather Price too, and his wife. Mr Price's sister married the schoolmaster's son from Bagpath, and you wouldn't believe it, he couldn't read or anything. If he had a letter or anything in the post he had to find someone who would read it to him, and hand it out to them. One of the people he got to read things for him was Mother. I don't know what was wrong with the woman courting him let alone marrying him. A kid from West Street, one of the Cleavers, took the house after the Prices left and worked from there as a builder. He used it as his yard.

Walkers lived in the end house. It had a way in and a proper yard and a cellar and a place for their horses. F & F Walker were the Tetbury hauliers, all with horses and carts. One of their horses was called Violet. It stood across the stable door all night and it sort of sat on a chain. They had to cover Violet's eyes and face up when they put it into the field, or it would jump the hedge and get into a new field.

When they took the sulphur out of the gasworks in Coombers Mead Walkers took it with a horse and cart and buried it in a little field that wasn't a field - a useless sort of place, all muddle hole - in Upton Road, just before you turn down the lane to Chavenage. They would cart the sulphur up there, where Vaizey's quarry is now. Fancy, they thought it was rubbish. Sulphur was waste at that time, and now it's used in the sugar industry, and with hops, and rubber. I worked at a sulphur mill, Alfred Smith's, in Hull, after I left baking, for years before I retired. It was a dirty job, but you were never black, and it was healthy, especially good for your skin. Now that Vaizey's quarry has come up to Upton Road from Chavenage Lane, they may find a bundle of sulphur there and wonder how it got there. I could tell them!

The last house in Upton Road, and the last house in Tetbury, was Wisteria Cottage where the Waltons lived, on the left, past the field, further down the road. Mr Walton was the gardener at Upton Grove, working for Squire Harding. Alf Davis, who was a carpenter for Holborows, lived there after they left. Wisteria Cottage had a water tank on the other side of the road, where Alf built himself a house later, with a pump to get the water across the road to another tank. That's where they got the water they used. Nobody had water laid on.

At the back of each house there was an outhouse and privies. The privies were very nice. One of ours was a two-holer.

Ball who lived in the house Under Bath Bridge (his house has been knocked down and a new one built) used to look after the privies. We used to enjoy ourselves when he was at work and we were coming down Hampton Street, because you could smell it! Then we knew that Mr Ball was earning his wages! He got paid to clean privies out at night. Mr Ball was the ganger of all the Town Council men. When he cleaned the privies he was doing a bit for himself. It's funny, isn't it? He must have been greedy! Edith wrote a poem about him and sent it to Mr Brown at the Council Offices - only a young man then; he was Fred Hills' cousin:

> 'Neighbour Ball - now don't turn pale -
> Although his preference is for ale
> Has even sewer water drunk.....'

Before he was due Dad used to dig a pit in the garden, and when Mr Ball cleaned the privies out Dad would bury it all in the pit and leave it for a long time until it was clean manure. Of course, everybody had the same. And we had a lot of manure from the road as well, and that's why everything in the garden was so good. There was a great depth of soil there, which is surprising when you think of all the stone for all the houses in Upton Road that came out of Vaizey's quarry just down the road. There must have been stone underneath the garden.

At the back of the privies there was the black iron bath, made of sheets of iron. We always bathed in it, two of us together. It was catching rainwater from the roof of the houses all the time, and we put hot water in it, too, from the boiler at the side of the fire. It wasn't always ours. I think it was something my dad picked up. When we needed it we carried it indoors (it wasn't as heavy as it looked) into the back room and filled up the boiler and lit the fire for hot water.

The boiler was for the clothes, of course it was: you used to boil clothes to get them clean in those days. The other thing it was used for was boiling puddings. Every so often we would have a pudding. There was a big basin and it was filled with any fruit you could get and covered with pastry and everything wrapped up in a cloth and put to boil; you would pull it out several times by the cloth to see how it was getting on. At the end you pulled it out by the cloth again, unwrapped the cloth, and turned it upside down on a big dish so the pastry was underneath. That was smashing! Especially the Christmas pudding! You forget that it was years ago! We had some big bowls - one was an ordinary bowl and the other was a brass preserving pan - and we would put all the stuff, the ingredients, in them, and Mother would light the fire under the boiler. We made the Christmas pudding mainly from the fruit we grew in the garden, so it cost nothing. The mixing of the pudding was done in the ordinary bowl, and when we had finished stirring it we turned it on to a big cloth and tied it up and boiled it in the water until it was done. The longer it was boiling for, the darker it got.

The first thing I remember is getting washed in the pantry, in cold water. Of course there was no way of heating water except in the kettle and that sat on the fire and took all day to get hot. You wouldn't use it to get washed, and that's why we washed in cold water. Then when we were getting washed we didn't have a light there, only a candle. And later my father made the oil light, worked on paraffin, to hang on the ceiling - he made it himself, you know.

My Dad had a couple of rose bushes because when they would be putting buds in, wherever, he could sneak one. That was in the front garden. Apart from the roses, we had capers there for flowers. People couldn't afford to buy roses and other plants and you had to have what you could get.

Of course most of the garden, front and back (the front garden was much bigger than it is now) was for food, and we had cabbages that you could cut and leave to grow on the stalk, sprouting stuff that you could keep on picking. That's how people had to live - we had no money and we had to grow all our food. But we put a lot back into it, and that's something that people can't do like that now.

It's a different world! It isn't one of our family, but someone else is doing our job, picking up horse manure at the top of Long Street to take home. Notice the dog lying in the road on the right.

I always say that gardens and fields need manure. And when I was a boy I used to go out and collect from the horses that came down the road. Of course all the traffic on Upton Road was horses and carts, and we would start just outside the house, collecting the manure, and we could go all the way down the road, and all the way to Tetbury, and we would be collecting up the manure.

Dad made us a cart, a proper cart, and one of us had to be the horse. We went up and down the road with it to collect manure for the garden. The manure was all up the road. It was like when cars changed gear, they used to spill a splash of oil on the road. The horses were like that, only it was manure, and very useful in the garden. We would fill the cart up with manure. When we were playing with it we took turns at being the horse, and the other had to pick up the manure. All the birds used to fly down to peck at the manure, especially goldfinches, because the horses were fed on corn. We would bring it back and it all went on the garden. It was a different world.

Well, I'll tell you. I don't mind the smell of cows and horses. The smell of their manure brings me to ecstasy, thinking about Gloucestershire. But I hate pig manure. Do you know what's best for cabbages? Our water - human water! I don't mean you do it on the cabbages, but save it and water the ground with it.

The back garden was all for food. Not just cabbage! We had chickens and 39 rabbits at one time. My father made brick huts, and roofs of galvanised iron that he had put through the clothes mangle. We sold a buck rabbit - he could stand right up against the fence - to Prides for breeding. It was a Flemish Giant. We got ten shillings for him. Ten shillings!

We had two goats once. I had to walk the first goat all the way past Chavenage, to Ledgemore, to be serviced and walk it back again on a rope. That one had eight pints of milk a day, though it was ever so small, and the young one we ate. Mr Vick came and killed it, and my Dad used saltpetre and made a rug for the floor from its skin. My father did a lot of work at the water tower in Blind Lane (of course there was a waterworks person as well) and he got permission to keep his goats there and they ate all the grass and rubbish where they were tethered.

We kept the goats up at the waterworks because they would eat all the garden - they ate all the ivy on the walls, and the bark on the trees. It is funny how we used to go on. A good job they weren't billy goats, like the one Alf Davis had (I have no idea what he thought he was going to do with a billy goat). With a billy you have to be careful or it will bunt you. You have to be the boss.

We had every sort of currants, raspberries, more than one kind, and strawberries. At the bottom of the garden there was a row of nut trees with big round nuts, bigger than the other hazel nuts but the same sort. We had gooseberries and blackcurrants and redcurrants and whitecurrants, loads of them. My father had a strange habit: he liked to eat blackcurrants cooked without any sugar. He really enjoyed them.

We had a quince tree in our garden. It wasn't in our garden at first, it was in next door's garden, Medcroft's, but when they moved and then Hortons moved we took their house as well and then it was our garden. It was a big tree and it had big fruit on it like a pear, a very big pear. But you couldn't eat it. It wasn't any good to eat; you had to chop it up and cook it first.

We had greengages in our garden too, and next door Mrs Medcroft had another one that was sweeter. When we moved next door, the tree was still there, but we found that it wasn't Mrs Medcroft's tree at all - it was next door again, in Price's garden, up against the wall.

If you have plenty of room for fruit you're all right. The best tree was the Victoria plum. You can't beat a Victoria plum, and they were great big ones like this! At the beginning of the first world war I was only eight, but as it went on and on I thought I would have to go. Dad was supposed to go to join the Army on the Monday, and he spent Sunday walking round the Victoria plum tree and saying goodbye to everyone while we sat around and had our fill. In the morning he went off to enlist. But he came back, rejected because of some impediment. I think he may have swallowed a piece of iron!

The Victoria was the best one, but we had a yellow one, too, behind Dad's shed. Next to that tree was the mealy yellow plum - you never see anything like it now. Edith's mother, Mrs Metcalfe, when she came to stay, she would stand under it, picking the plums and eating them.

There was another unusual tree, one that you don't often see, and that was a medlar. There used to be another one in the garden behind The Ferns in Long Street, that became the Grammar School. A medlar is like a quince - can't eat it when it is ripe. You have to wait with a medlar until it is almost rotten - they say 'as rotten as a medlar'. We used to call them 'open-ass'. The tree at The Ferns was always full of fruit. I don't know whether the kids at the school had them.

At the bottom of the garden there was a field belonging to Mr Lewis the baker. All the beautiful blackberries that were there! Mr Lewis didn't want them and he wanted to keep people out of his field and he cut them down, but they grew up stronger. He would say 'Tisn't theirs, they shan't have them!' But we did.

There used to be a sort of layby outside number 4 Upton Road that was made so that the landlord could put his pony and trap off the road when he came to collect the rents. His name was Mr Lewis too, and he used to come over from Beverstone, where he lived. I never knew who owned that little piece of land and I'm not sure what has happened to it. There was a heap of earth that was dug out to make it, that Medcrofts used as a flower garden. That's gone, too. Most of it is a driveway for a car to come in now; you can still see a bit of the wall curving where the bay was, to the right of the gate to number 4.

Sometimes the landlord's wife came to collect the rent instead of him, and when the good lady was there she would wander down the garden and help herself to things there - fruit and so on. Rude of her, wasn't it? They had a garden of their own. Once she even went down with a basket and filled it with apples from our tree. After that my dad built an extra fence at the back of the house to stop her getting through.

These Lewises went to the Zoar chapel by The Green. They had plenty of money, and they owned a lot of houses. Our four - numbers 1 to 4 - were half a crown a week each. It seems amazing now that it was worth calling for ten shillings for the four houses.

After the Hortons left and their house next door was empty we took it over for us boys to sleep in, and Dad bored a hole right through the dividing wall and put a proper speaking tube in, in case we were ill or anything and needed to call him or Mother in the night. We boys slept at number 4 and went to bed with the doors wide open. Dad used the living room of number 4 as a workshop. Sometimes I had a bit of money and I put it in that room to hide it from the others, but Dad always found it and hid it from me.

He made all sorts of things at work, at Witchell's, everything that you would buy ready made nowadays. For instance at work he made lids for all kinds of pots, and lids for milk churns, and he made things at home too, in his workshop. He made a milk-can in there, as good as you could buy anywhere.

Later my father made the oil light, worked on paraffin, to hang on the ceiling - he made it himself, you know; and at one time he made a gas light, a lamp that went on the chimney.

I don't suppose many people have had a gasholder actually in their garden! We did, because just before the first world war Dad built a gas lighting system for our house that ran on acetylene, and the gas that was produced was stored in the back garden at home. He took the pigsty when it was cleaned out (we never had pigs) and he built his own gasworks in it with a proper gasholder. It worked on carbide and water - it just dripped and kept going like that and we had gaslight for the first time. He made everything himself, of course he did. It worked straight off when he had got it done.

He had just got it nicely going when the war came, and in the war there was a shortage of carbide. We couldn't get any and that was the end of the gasworks. But he built all that himself.

Later, a door was cut through between the two sculleries as well, so we could walk through without going outside. But what amazed me when it was done was the thickness of the wall between the two houses.

So we had both houses and we used to keep our bikes (when we had them) downstairs at number 4, in the living room, and there was the landing and one bedroom. Now, there wasn't any electricity in those days, and if you wanted a light upstairs you had to take a candle. Eddie and I had the bedroom, but we didn't have a candle, and we had to go up and get undressed and into bed in the dark.

Eddie and I went upstairs this evening in the dark as usual; we left the front door open (we never shut the door) and went up the stairs. Usually the bedroom door was kept open, too, but this night it was windy and the door had shut. I expect it had blown to.

Well, we opened the door and there was this horrible noise: Whussh! we shut the door quickly and ran downstairs. There wasn't anybody else about so we went round the back of the house - we were sure there was a burglar - and got two big sticks, and crept back into the house and upstairs. We stood at the top of the stairs and very quietly opened the door and rushed in. Whussh! it went again, very loud, and it was completely dark. We stood there with our sticks, because nobody moved in the room, and then there was a little bit of light, enough to see that there was nobody there, and then there was a very little Whussh! and we could see what it was.

The room had been papered and the paper was beginning to come off the wall.

When the door opened, a big piece of paper had lifted up and whusshed against the wall. We were relieved that it wasn't a burglar, but we thought we had done well, especially if it had been.

There's another story about when we were sleeping in that house. At first two of us, and then three, were sleeping in the same bed. It was a nice bed, and one night, when there were three of us going to bed, we had a candle. Well, we got into bed, and we hadn't blown the candle out, and somehow we flopped the bedclothes over the candle. The next thing, we had a bonfire in bed!

One day there were two or three of us boys in number 4, waiting for the storm to pass. It was raining and thundering. Now if there was a thunderstorm we always opened the back door and the front door - well, you know the front door was open anyway. A thunderbolt came in through the front door and straight past us and out the back door - it shot in and flashed in the house and shot out again - and went down the garden and over into the field. It flashed in the field and tore the turf up there.

Dad bought the two houses from the landlord before he retired and Raymond bought both houses, and number 1 and number 2, after he had Gale's shop in Long Street.

After we had all left home Rene and her husband Billy Lewis had number 4.

All the stone for the houses, and the tiles on the roofs, came from Vaizey's quarry in Chavenage Lane. Other roof tiles came from the quarry at Bath Road (that quarry was on land belonging to Mr Hedges).

I well remember this picture being taken. I am standing on the stool on the left, wearing Hector Walton's clothes.

There is a photograph that was taken outside the house. I remember it being taken very well. There is a stool at the front that my Dad made. Raymond is sitting on it in the picture. My Dad is wearing a bowler hat and a collar and tie, and Clarence is sitting on his knee wearing a dress - all little boys wore dresses then. Laura, the next youngest, is sitting on Mother's knee. Vera, the eldest, is at the back on the right, Olive is in the middle, and I am on the left. But it wasn't me at all, you know. Well, it was me, but the clothes all belonged to Hector Walton at Wisteria, just down the road, or they had belonged to him recently.

Rene with her doll. She was not in the family photograph because she had gone to live at Chedworth when it was taken. The National School forgot to make a note in the register that she had left. I suppose they are still marking her absent.

I was wearing his semi-stiff collar like the Eton children wore; I had his knickerbockers, done up like that, you know, and the coat. Hector Walton was a bit older than me. The Waltons and our family were friendly, but they were well off. They lived at Wisteria Cottage, which was one house then with a big garden. It was the gardener's house for Upton Grove, and Mr Walton was the head gardener. There was an older brother, but I can't remember his name - he was friendly with Reg Boulton next door - and the eldest was a girl called Annie. She was a lovely girl with beautiful long hair all the way down her back to her bottom. She won a medal for her hair, for years. I don't know whether the boys are alive, but I know where Annie is - in New Church Street graveyard, quite near our family.

Our Eddie was in the army during the war and at the end when he came out he was sent to be fitted for a suit - what they called the demob suit - and he was somewhere to do with the War Department. He had to give his name: Edmund Peters. 'Do you know anyone called Frank Peters?' the man said.

'He's my brother!' Eddie said. It was Hector Walton, working for the War Department.

I remember a lot of things well, from when I was very little, younger than I am in that photograph.

Did you know what I was supposed to have said when I first spoke? I don't remember, but this is what they always told me: 'Eat that now!' I suppose being interested in food is a family characteristic, and I was showing it early.

I had a hoop to play with. We all had some sort of a hoop, but this one was made by Dad out of iron. I had one of my own and I think one of the others had one that he made, too. There was a hook on the handle and the hoop and the stick were made together, and you had to hold the stick in your hand to hold the hoop. The hoop was made of iron and it stood as tall as that! It was professionally made. You used to run with your hoop. When you began you put the hook of the handle low down and just touched the hoop - it was iron against iron - as a means of pushing it, and when it was going you had to run with it. That was when there were two of us boys who could run with a hoop - really little kids didn't get up to things like that.

When I was little at Upton Road a man got killed on a horse and someone cut a cross on a stone in the wall and painted it red. If they haven't knocked that wall down it's still there.

Tetbury was very quiet in those days. Before I began to go to school I was at home all day with Mother. Now, when I was very little I think the only person in Tetbury who had a car was Doctor Mellish. When he set out on his rounds, calling on patients, you could hear the car start up in New Church Street.

Another thing is that on the other side of the road, coming out of Tetbury from the Picket Harp, there wasn't a pavement but there was a kind of kerb laid sideways between the grass and the roadway. When Vera came from school she used to cross over the road from Chavenage Lane and walk on the stones. Well, I always could hear her when she was coming up the road and I would say 'Vera's coming!'

My father died walking along there.

We always had a stack of firewood. I suppose Dad would cut it up, but Mother went with a horse and cart and collected it from where they were cutting down trees. She brought the whole tree back except for the trunk. When Mother was young, before she was married, she had a horse of her own to ride. She fell off it a lot, she said, but she was always used to horses.

We had a well, a beautiful well, like a big room with cement all round, and we used to clean it out once a year, but it was the water off the roof. Plenty of water, but there had been all these sparrows on the roof! Anyway, you left the water there a long time and all the sediment went down to the bottom. When it rained a lot and there was plenty of water it was clear. The ladder to get into the well was kept in a box. It was quite a job to clean the well out because of all the sediment. We had a filter in the pantry. The water was poured in the top and came out at the bottom. They said it was like Kruschen salts.

It was the well for four houses, and there was an art, a skill, in getting water out of it. Mrs Medcroft next door had real skill - throw the bucket in, skilfully turn it over until it sank, and then pull it straight out on its rope. We all used it for washing and drinking, but Mrs Medcroft didn't like to use it when she was doing other people's washing.

I went down to the fountain in London Road to get water for Mrs Medcroft because she was washing. She was a washerwoman. Well, I don't know, but I always used to go for it. Now the fountain isn't there any more, is it? I always think you should never let go of any place where you can get water. But a lot of the water round Tetbury seems to have dried up - all down Chavenage Lane, for instance, and where it goes across Charlton Road.

We had one of these water carts with iron wheels - you've seen the dustman with things like it, swinging, like this one, just held like that, on a swivel, a barrel, a big one. It was a three-wheeler, two wheels at the front side by side. The gentry used to have things like that for watering the garden, before there were hosepipes: one man or a boy would push it round and take the water out for a watering can. And my father made that, too. You put a piece of wood like a cross on the top to stop the water splashing over.

Someone is walking up the hill carrying two buckets of water with a yoke over his shoulders. Not many people in Tetbury had their own water supply. Some used other people's wells or taps but some preferred to get their water out of a stream or a spring. The man in the picture may have filled his buckets from the stream under Bath Bridge. At Upton Road we kept our yoke in the kitchen.

Anytime I would do it. It was Fred's job, the son's job, but if I was handy I used to go.

We used to go to Tetbury for water for ourselves, you know, but more to the tap in the street by Coombers Mead. I used to go down with a yoke and two buckets for the water we drank. The tap was right on the corner at the top of Hampton Street. Look, you looked right across at the police station, or Purnells, from there: it was on the corner of New Church Street, by Elgin House. It was a Scotsman, you know, who lived there, Macdonald, that had the garage up in Long Street. The tap wasn't outside his house, it was on the corner of the pavement where you come down Hampton Street to town, then you turn there into New Church Street, and that's where the tap was.

Another thing I used to do, I used to fetch water from the tap by Mr Macdonald's house for the lady at the corner house opposite, the house on the corner of New Church Street.

It was a funny life! Her name was Mrs Holland. If you saw her you'd be frightened because she made up that much! When you got there she wouldn't open the door for you, just a little bit; she would put one empty bucket round the door like that, and then another. I would give them to her full one at a time through the door that she hardly opened. She didn't have a tap or a well, you see. A lot of those houses didn't.

I knew all about her, but I don't know how I came to get the water for her. Life's too complicated! They knew I was willing. I got the water every time I went round, when I went to school and things like that. Life was different altogether to what it is now. Everything, there's never anything the same now that there used to be. Ay.

Mrs Holland used to hit her boys, Guy and John, over the head with a pan. Remember about Guy and the ten shilling note? If he had lost it she would have given him a good hiding.

You didn't get paid for doing things like that, getting water! Nobody thought much about paying: there was no thought of paying really. You didn't give a kid half a crown or a motorbike for going shopping or anything like that. Now, I'll tell you. It was always Mrs Medcroft, if I went for water she would give me a penny or a piece of cake.

I used to prefer the cake. I used to say, 'But I'd like a piece of cake!' which of course was sensible, and so she would say, 'Oh, you do know what you do like. You say the best, don't you?' Life's different altogether to what it is now. Everything, there's never anything the same now that there used to be.

Almost the last time I was in Tetbury they told me 'Fred Medcroft's in hospital.' I was very hesitant about going to see him; I was nervous; I didn't know whether he could see me; I didn't know how ill he was. Anyrate, I did go and see him. I went up to the hospital there, and asked, 'Can I see Mr Medcroft?' and I got to the door of the ward, and I wondered again, should I go in? But I knocked and went in, and there was one old man in the bed.

'Hello, Fred,' I said.

'Well, that's all right,' he said, 'who are you?'

I knew I wouldn't recognise him and he didn't recognise me. I told you, when we were boys, and he got a job at The Priory stables in London Road opposite the gasworks, where the hotel is now, I used to help him there and get water.

Anyrate I told him who I was, and he knew me by what I said.

He said, 'Thank you a thousand times for coming to see me.'

I'm glad I saw him.

The last time I met his mother she was well over eighty and still living in Chavenage Lane where they moved to from 4 Upton Road, and still going out to work in people's houses. 'What are you doing that for?' I asked.

'I'm saving for my old age,' she said. She was working hard because she didn't want to go in the workhouse!

When I was a young man I didn't seem to be interested in girls. 'Ah, Frank,' Mrs Medcroft used to say, 'you wait till Miss Right comes along!'

'Tommy likes a bit of bread and butter, doesn't he, Other?' That was Tommy Medcroft, Mrs Medcroft's grandson (he couldn't say Mother then). She had heaps of grandchildren, more than one of them called Tommy.

I'll tell you something else about her: she used to make turdovers(!).

Of course, Upton Road is part of Hampton Street now, but Hampton Street used to stop after the pike house, before Chavenage Lane, and it was all fields all the way to Avening except for the row of houses where I lived.

I was born and brought up in Upton Road. The first house is number 1, then 2,3 and 4. We lived at number 3 and then 4 as well. Now those two houses are 78 and 80 Hampton Street but Upton Road was a separate hamlet then.

At the division of Chavenage Lane and Upton Road there is a high wall and behind the wall there used to be one house, and a man called Spider lived there, who worked for the saddler. Warners had relatives who lived there at a different time. I remember a Mrs Warner.

They built Oxleaze Lane when the houses were built there, not long before the second war, but there was one house that was on the road where they built the way through. The busiest man in Tetbury was Mr Harmer, the Town Clerk or something like that, who lived there. Young Brown got the job after him. That was the first house after the corner of Chavenage Lane. And there was one more house that belonged to Mr

Hudson, a teacher. We called him Tabby Hudson, and he lived opposite the Picket Harp.

We went into all the houses while they were being built from town up to the Picket Harp. The first ones were built when I was little. We never did any damage.

And I watched the man build the wall there, too.

When I was a boy there used to be a lot of tramps. When they left the workhouse Casual Ward in the morning they would call at houses and ask for some hot water to make tea, and hope they would get the tea as well, and perhaps something to eat. They say they used to make marks on the house that other tramps would recognise to show whether people were kind to them or not.

Now at one time there was a police constable, a horrible man, Mrs Kidd's grandson in law, who lived near the church. He used to hang about near the top of Gumstool Hill in the morning to see if a tramp came out at the usual time. If he did, he would follow him through Tetbury and walking out on the road, and the policeman would be behind the tramp all the way, to make sure he didn't go begging.

Sometimes a tramp would come out of Tetbury and up Upton Road, walking, and behind him there would be this policeman. He used to march past the houses behind the tramp hoping he would try to beg. But I don't think he ever got a catch.

If my mother saw the tramp (and remember, she never closed the front door) she would call out to him, 'Would you like a cup of tea?' And if he said 'Yes,' she would say 'Come indoors, and shut the door behind you.' That was so that the policemen couldn't see him. You would think the police wouldn't have anything to do, would you? They probably hadn't!

Once she was very upset by a tramp. She called him in and she offered him some food to take away with him. But she thought he didn't want food, he wanted her to give him some money. But she never gave money to tramps - she never had any money! He took the parcel of food from her and went off towards Stroud. We found the food thrown over a wall. That was horrible when you didn't have too much to give away.

There were walnut trees all round the Rec, or Cook's field as it was, and in Joe Roseblade's garden at the pike house, and the gardens of two other houses by there, and at Bignells, down Chavenage Lane. Uncle Austin had one at Crossroads in Shipton Moyne. I think my cousin Lily still has it. We used to get walnuts and put them green in a hole in the garden in summer and dig them up much later. When we dug them up in the winter, when we opened the ground, the hoods dropped off and we would eat them. That was our happy Christmas, with an orange and an ice mouse!

You had to be sharp getting your walnuts. Crows will strip the flipping trees until they have eaten everything, and then they pull wheat from the ricks and eat that. When I was working in Hull I took a walnut to work with me, to the bakehouse, and the lad I was working with said 'Where did you get that?'

'I picked it,' I said, 'from a tree at home.'

'You can't pick them,' he said. 'They come from Greece!' He didn't know there were hazelnuts in England, either, and I brought him some of those, too.

The road past our house was the main road to Gloucester. The road was much narrower then. It could only take one horse and cart at a time, and with that much pavement - there was about a foot - they could just get one past the other. And there were trees all along Upton Road. Beautiful elm trees went both sides of the road from the corner of Chavenage Lane all the way along Upton Road to Bert Slade's, and then all the way down on the other side, down to Wisteria Cottage. Many birds nested in the trees. The trees were full of birds.

People used to walk everywhere, you know. People used to go there for a walk under the elm trees, for pleasure. Men used to walk up Upton Road in their lunchtime, just for exercise. I often used to wonder myself, What do they want to do that for? because I was always doing things, and the last thing I could think of doing was going for a walk as well.

Charlie Brown and his brothers and sisters had the field opposite our house in Upton Road, or Hampton Street as they call it now, and there was a high stone wall with one elm tree growing out of the top and then the field above the road, with the row of elm trees all the way down to Wisteria.

One time they cut most of the elm trees down, and in the end there wasn't but one, and that was the one opposite our house.

The wall was on Charlie Brown's land and the tree must have been growing through the wall. It had got dangerous: whenever there was a wind it rocked to and fro and we thought it might bring the wall down and block the road and perhaps damage our house. In the end Eddie and another man sawed that tree down. I think the rest of the trees had all been cut down by then for the wood. Someone made a lot of money. I think that's why they had them all down, because it was before the road was widened. There used to be the last few stumps left for years at the bottom of the hill. I don't know where the birds have all gone. They went when they cut the trees down.

Then they came to widen the road. Our garden was quite long, and opposite our house was the high wall where the tree had been growing out of the top. They took a big piece of our garden, and removed the wall on the other side, and made a wide verge and a steep grassy bank. That made the road wide enough for lorries and buses. The council estate was being built beyond the bank by Holborows. Later they altered the slope of the hill, too.

All boys and young men used to climb trees, and all the elm trees got climbed again and again. Eddie was the most magnificent climber. One day he was climbing the tree opposite with several of his friends - one of them was Guy Holland from the corner of Long Street and New Church Street, someone we always played with - when along came Charlie Brown, carrying a switch, and caught them all up there. 'Come down out of my tree, you boys!' And they all came down, and he whipped them all with the switch. All except Eddie, that is because Eddie pretended he was stuck up the tree, and couldn't get down. He was too delicate, and it was too difficult. All the time he was working his way along thinner and thinner branches, from smaller branches to the outside branches; and Charlie Brown was telling him to come down, and all the time Eddie was saying he couldn't get down, and in the end he was at the end of a long branch that hung right down over the road, clear of the wall, and Charlie Brown was still standing on the wall, and Eddie dropped off the branch into the middle of the road and ran away. He was the only one who didn't get whipped!

Eddie was fly, really fly. He was a great climber. He used to climb on top of the house roof too, and he could get right up to the chimney pot.

Once, when Mr Horton was away at the war, it had been snowing, and Eddie climbed on Horton's roof and dropped snowballs down the chimney.

Another day he went after the hawk's nest. He went up the elm tree to get the hawk's egg, one branch after another, until he couldn't manage any more. But he had the long rope with him, and he threw it up and used it. He slung it over a strong branch and climbed up the rope, and then he did that again, and that's how he got to the hawk's nest and found one egg. Every boy had a cap on his head in those days, and Eddie put the egg behind the peak of his cap. It was a bright reddy-coloured egg, beautiful.

Eddie would get anywhere. There were lime trees all around the garden at Wisteria, very hard to climb. He used to get Dad's six-inch iron nails and hammer them in, and climb up that way. When those trees were cut down they must have had some bother with the nails! Dad used to make clouts at Witchell's for nailing floorboards - that was one of the jobs he did - but he bought the six-inch nails. Now most of those trees have gone, too. They tell me it's illegal to climb trees now.

I'll tell you something from the first world war that was exciting for us lads. I mean me and Eddie and Raymond - Clarence was too little, and wouldn't have been into anything like it. It must have been during the very early part of the first world war. We knew about aeroplanes, but there were no planes to be seen and none of us had seen one. All boys were making model aeroplanes out of thick cardboard and pins. We made model planes when we hadn't even seen one. Some of our early ones didn't look much like aeroplanes.

One day we were at home, and we heard the sound of an aeroplane and we looked up, and there it was, going overhead very low, and we thought it was landing in the field.

'It's by us! right by us!'

We all rushed out and down the road but it carried on past Wisteria and we all ran after it. We thought he had crossed over the road because it looked as if he was going to the right. We carried on towards Upton, and on - you know where you first see the church spire when you're coming from Avening? Well, if you were coming from Avening it would be the field on the right just there. The plane was in the field by Keevil's Farm, and it was the pilot's father's farm. He came down by his father's house, over from France. The aeroplane was there for some time, because of officialdom.

In those days you had to have two people, because it took two to start it. One man couldn't go until the other man had turned the propellor. One of them shouted 'Contact!' and then 'Switch!' and the second person had to give the propellor a tug, and then it didn't go and they had to do it again, and that time it went. It was very interesting. Sometimes nothing happened, but if it started it would go ddr-ddr-ddr and then BBBBBBBBBBBBBBRRR! I heard that noise for the first time at Upton.

We watched them. There were two of them in the plane. One held the propellor in his hand and turned it a bit and then he shouted 'Contact!' and the other one said 'On!' - it didn't half sound businesslike - and then he turned the propellor again and there was the noise, and then it started. That was the first plane I ever saw.

Afterwards we used to make planes out of pins and cardboard. We had a better idea of aeroplanes after the one that came down at Upton. Real ones were made out of wood and all covered with cloth, all the fuselage, where you would expect metal, thick cloth, painted. We always used to take our improved models to the field by Keevil's Farm to fly them.

Keevil's farm was up towards Major Little's: Keevil caught Eddie in his field once and he said 'What's your name?' and Eddie said 'Peters, Sir,' and Keevil said 'Well, Peterson, get along home!' You see, he didn't know him and he thought he said Peterson. Eddie went home and told us, and of course Mr Keevil couldn't be everywhere at once, and we knew we weren't supposed to be there - you're not allowed to go on a farm, you know - and as you would expect we went back there as often as we could.

There wasn't any margarine in those days, and we never had butter on our bread. We always had dripping, beautiful dripping, and we used to get it from the kitchen at Upton Grove. Squire Harding at Upton Grove had a chauffeur, a man called Seal, but he liked walking and used the car rarely. We would ask Mother for fourpence, and take a basket and a basin, and we looked out for him walking. We would go round to the kitchen of his house with the fourpence and buy a bowl of dripping. The dripping was perks for the cook. We paid her fourpence for the pound of dripping, and she put it in the basin. When we met Squire Harding we saluted him. He would say, 'Hello, what have you there?'

'Dripping, sir.'

'How much did you pay for it?'

'Fourpence, sir.'

'Oh, too dear, too dear.'

And he would reach his hand into his pocket and give me the money back - but he didn't know I had a cake at the bottom of the basket, under the dripping!

Mother worked there, in the garden at Upton Grove, too. Poor lady, she never had anything to eat. She used to see me off at six o'clock after she had made sure that I had something to eat and a drink of something, of course, and then she went straight off to work.

There were three houses belonging to Upton Grove where the gardener, the chauffeur and the bailiff lived. Mrs Hayes the bailiff's wife sold eggs, thirteen to the dozen. They had a daughter called Ethel who was a bright spark with the boys. She went to live on Romney Marsh.

Squire Harding's car was a Renault, made in 1906, the year after I was born. It came to me like a shot that I knew the car, and I had quite a shock when I remembered it. I remember Mr Seal the chauffeur; I was a friend of his son Ronald. The car had a whistle fixed in the exhaust pipe instead of a horn, and you could hear it whistling as it came down the road. It worked when the chauffeur pulled a string. It was quite a loud whistle. The glass of the windscreen didn't go right to the top, and the windscreen wiper was a hand one. Mr Seal sat outside, and he pushed and pulled the wiper to and fro across the winsdscreen. He had to do it by hand. That was before there were any kind of mechanical wipers. The wheels had a rim with a tyre attached, like you would have the spare wheel but it was only the rim and a tyre. It had John Bull tyres. The car had two little oil lamps at the side and one big acetylene lamp in front. Squire Harding didn't go anywhere in it. He used to send Mr Seal with the car to the station to pick people up. The car didn't go out of Tetbury you know. It's probably still at the house.

Lowsley-Williams at Chavenage House had a little car, too. Theirs had a back part that would take a parcel or two. Nowadays you might call it a pick-up, but it was only two seats and a parcel shelf, and they only used it to go to the station.

It was in their yard for years. It lay there with a lot of old iron stuff that had been put aside. I used to go up there with bread and it was still there when I left Tetbury in 1947 to work for Jackson's in Hull.

Upton House was where Major Little and Lady Guendolene lived. That's a very big house. Occasionally they had their house cleaned, and the way of it was a van would arrive outside, and in the van was a motor, like a vacuum cleaner. A long tube ran from the motor all round the house, and they swept it from the ground up, taking the tube upstairs when they had done downstairs. The van stopped there all day until they had finished the job. That was before people had electricity, even rich people. I thought, many times, What if anything was lurking around in the house - suck - and it would be gone! Say, a ring on a dressing table, or whatever. That's my naughty mind!

There was one thing I could do and I could do it well. I used to be able to imitate animals, the noises they make, like talking to them. I have been in Wales at a gate of a field of sheep or cows and talked to them and they have come over to me. I have done it on holiday in different places. They must understand the way we talk in Gloucestershire - they must have come from Tetbury! I only did it for fun, you know; when there were children about I would do it. The cockerel was my best one, but cats was good too. One day I was outside the house in Upton Road, by the window, and I was doing two cats quarrelling, and very quietly my sister Olive was creeping up on me with a bucket of water - she thought there really were two cats outside! I nearly got the water all over me.

I could do people, too, as well as animals. One I remember was a Scotchman, a preacher: he read out the whole of the first verse of a hymn, and I still remember it - but only in his voice.

People think you're telling lies about that time. It's like a foreign country. For an instance, there was a big iron sailor at number 3, holding the front door open. We had a crate of drinks in the hot weather and we used to sell them from the house to people going past. We had a notice up on a post: MINERAL WATERS FOR SALE. We sold pop in bottles with a round glass marble stopper. They were the sort of bottles that you opened by pushing your finger down on the stopper. Olive showed us how to do it. Well, once Olive had shown us how, we used to take a drink out of the bottle. There used to be a lot of sunshine all the time in those summers. It was hot and they were short of water every year. One year they shot at the clouds but it didn't do much good.

When we weren't selling pop we would go gleaning in the fields for wheat, Mother and the children, after the harvest. There was corn and straw lying on the ground. We retrieved it all in the end. The weather was always better - it was fine all the time. We were out all the summer holidays with Mother, doing the wheat she collected in the field from gleaning - and before, and after.

One of the fields we always gleaned in was the one called Witchell's Field, but there were different places. One was on Barrett's Hill, on the right beyond the Folly.

That was a place you could see foxes and their young in the field.

When we went gleaning in the field we took all our bits and bobbles with us, such as our bows and arrows, and played cowboys and indians all out in the field as well as working. One year we found our bows and arrows from when we shouldn't have been there earlier in the year. There were some people called Bird used to come out with us, and Pills, and the Crews. During the war there was always us and the three other families went gleaning. There were other families too.

Many years later I went to the Open Brethren meeting in Hampton Street and I met a young woman there called Lucy Crew. She was one I had met gleaning wheat. I mentioned it to her, and she remembered.

After we had finished gleaning and taken everything home, the miller came in that day and tapped on your door. He ground your corn into flour, and he took so much of it to pay. His name was Mr Bird. But we didn't give him all of it. We kept a lot of the corn we gleaned and fed the hens and the animals with it. I went down and fed pigs with a couple of buckets of the barley we had gleaned and I used to make pig noises at them.

I don't know now how it happened, but Eddie and I got a bike. It may have been thrown away. It was broken right through the bottom bracket, and it might not have been any use at all. Can you guess what happened? It was my father who put it all together, and it worked all right after that. We both used to ride it and make it go as fast as possible, which wasn't very fast. But the important thing is this: it was the first bicycle (apart from Dad's) that was ever seen in Upton Road.

When we were out playing along Upton Road we boys used to meet Mr Calcott. There would be two of us, me and Eddie, and he would have been down from Avening to Tetbury on his beautiful Dursley Pedersen bicycle, all wires, for a drink. He had a job with the Government, something to do with money and currency, and he lived at the Lodge at the top of Tetbury Hill. 'Did you see Calcott?' we would say - that's Eddie and me. So one of us would go right up the road, and when he came past you would put your hand to your hat. He would put his hand in his ticket pocket and throw out a sixpence. And then the same thing happened up the road. So we did well.

I mentioned that the Hortons lived next door. Well, a few years ago I met one of the Hortons. I had been sent to Doughton to look for a nursing home and when we got there I knew all the people but there wasn't a nursing home. I met a fellow with a stone lorry and I asked him, 'Do you know a nursing home?' He was a great big rough fellow, very pleasant.

'Who are you looking for?' he asked, and then he said 'My name's Horton.' I thought he wasn't capable of being with a wagon. He was about the same age as myself! 'I don't know any nursing home,' he said. 'Where are you from?'

'Tetbury, Upton Road.'

'That's where we lived.'

'There was George Horton next to us.'

'That's my dad!'

'Your dad! That's a long time ago now. Did he have any slight impediment? Can I do it? Would you mind if I showed you how he used to speak to me?' I did my imitation: 'Wotcher mate!'

'That's my dad!'

'Well, who are you?'

'Arthur.'

'I only remember one of the Hortons.'

'Who was that?'

'Wyndham.'

'He was in the Guards, but he's died.'

I never did find the nursing home.

My father used to go to the Greyhound in Hampton Street for a drink after he had finished gardening, around 9 o'clock most often. Sometimes when they lived next door I used to fetch Mrs Horton a pint of beer from the Greyhound, the Boultons, in her own bottle. She had a tumbler and she poured the beer out from the bottle, guggled it out into the glass, and put her lips together. It was a masterpiece, the way she poured that beer and drank it.

When she was drinking her beer, she would say: 'Go to sleep, Arbie, there's a good boy, and you shall have a toffee in the morning.' Of course, he never got a toffee. I didn't dare say that to this chap. He was Arbie!

There were three Horton brothers. One lived at Cutwell, Harry Horton, who drove a milk cart, one on the Knap (Gilbert, who was Hubert's father) and one, George, was her husband and lived at 4 Upton Road before our family took it over.

When George Horton was in the army (he was batman to a captain) Mrs Horton was so hard up that she broke up all the back panels out of the wooden furniture to use as firewood. She was very hard up, but she would have her beer.

Another of their sons was called George, too, and he was about my age. He was a stupid kid. He had a straw hat and he held it out for us to throw things in. The first stone went straight through the crown of his hat on to the road.

He was one of the boys I used to play with in Chavenage Lane on a Sunday afternoon. We used to go down to Chavenage Lane with the other boys and jump across the water and throw stones; and sometimes we would win a few apples. One day I went through a hole in Chavenage

Lane where the water used to flow underground by the Folly, with a candle on a piece of wood in front of me, up to the house and under the house and across the road. I pushed the piece of wood in front of me because I couldn't carry the candle. Fancy attempting such a thing as that! It was dry, but I expect I got mucky. If there had been anything in the way it would have been awkward. I couldn't crawl backwards. But I never thought of such a thing as that! I thought it was clever. Anyrate, the stream used to go under the house and into the field that way. There was usually too much water to have tried - it must have been the beginning of the drought.

There's a small copse on the other side of Chavenage Lane and in the middle there used to be an apple tree. We knew everything. We had all the apples, and ate them on our way round. And there were wild strawberries in Vaizey's quarry, and at blackberry time we boys would go with a walking stick and a tin bath with two handles, and the boys would go along the bushes just like that, and fill it right up with blackberries. I used to look lower down, where the fruit was down among the grass. I used to find the very sweet ones and I ate them. This was during the war. I don't remember what happened to the blackberries afterwards. We were supposed to be collecting blackberries for the military to use as colour. They said it was for dye, but I think it was something more sensible. I reckon they ate them. We used to take our bathful of blackberries to an army kitchen that was set up in New Church Street. I think I could show you more than I could tell you where it was. They paid us. Oh yes.

The water ran across in front of Mrs Medcroft's house in Chavenage Lane and down to Charlton Road and Cutwell and into the Arnold. It's strange there isn't water there. I've seen the Arnold water from side to side, and the next field from Bath Bridge. Mind, in summer there was often no water in the river past Bath Bridge. When we lived at 6 Bath Road, Edith wanted a stone wall built in the garden, and for a time I would go down to the river and pick up a stone or two, and that's how I built the wall across the garden. She grew little plants in it like aubretia and stonecrop. It wasn't a bad wall when I'd finished.

I don't know where all the water has gone now. I think when you have water you should look after it, and keep it.

There's one last thing about the house at Upton Road: long after I had left Tetbury my mother died, and after that the people who had the house had a sort of extension with big windows at the back, where my dad's lean-to for drying tobacco and the privies had been. It was like a conservatory and they could sit in their room and look into next door. I'm sure that wasn't right. People are hand in glove with the Council in Tetbury, and that's probably how it happened. Look at Witchell's, with a preservation order, and they hid it behind corrugated iron while they were knocking it down.

I was in Tetbury on holiday when they began to put scaffolding round the old Three Cups building that used to be Witchell's, in Church Street. Before we went home it had been demolished.

– THE FOURTH PART –

A Working Boy

I went to the school by the Knap. It isn't a school now, but we all went there except Rene who lived at Chedworth with our uncle and aunt. We all had white hair, you know, and they used to call us 'Snowdrop'. The school was called a National School then. Tetbury National School. It was the only school in Tetbury apart from some private ones.

It was all right in the babies' class, because all we did there was play with toys. I liked that!

I went to the school by the Knap, Tetbury National School, when I was four years old. The gaffer used to start ringing the bell just before nine o' clock and I got there every morning before it stopped, even when I was working before school.

Jackie Dance was the boss and his wife, Mrs Dance, took the first class in the infants' school. At first she taught us; and then Miss Abbott followed her. Mrs Dance was the Head Mistress of the infants' school but I thought she wasn't a teacher, just the Head Master's wife, and she was roped in. Then Miss Abbott, who died while I was there, had the baby class. Later there was Dorothy McCracken who married Alec Lewis the baker's son. Not long after I started in the infants' school it was the Coronation and we all got a mug. I still have mine in the cupboard.

There were two girls who were friends. One of them offered me a drink of lemonade out of a bottle, but it was wee! I didn't try it!

Mrs Dance, my teacher in the infants school, outside her house in New Church Street.

I used to be very interested in what we called grammar, and I remember some of the tricks: 'thee and thou, this and that, these that, each every, either neither, what are they?' Then there was 'a and the; this, that, these, those!' I remember, and I used to be so interested in it, but I couldn't get on. They're parts of the make-up of a sentence, aren't they?

It was grammar. That's what I learned. I learned some Shakespeare at school, but I learned that through listening to somebody else.

Jackie Dance was the gaffer in the boys' school when I was there first. Mr Dance was the School Master before Mr Webb. Poor old Jackie Dance! He had some peculiarities. Jackie Dance had a tuning fork and he would strike it and call: 'Doh! one, two!' We liked the way he held the tuning fork in his hand and he struck it on the desk and sang: 'Soh!!' The whole class would start off singing. We did a lot of singing. But we never sang 'Now the day is over And we're going home' because we only sang in the morning!

Another teacher came after Mr Dance, but not for long. I don't remember his name. He brought a fresh rule, not to speak while he was out of the room. If he caught anyone speaking he would thrash them: he said, 'If anyone talks while I am gone I will wallop them!' If he wanted to he could have begun a bit gentler than that. Well, he soon picked on a boy and it wasn't the right one, a boy called Raymond Beale. His father was a big man, and he went to the teacher's lodging that night, and the master didn't turn up in the morning. He went away again.

After that we got Mr Webb. That would be about the end of the war. He was a nasty fellow who used to pinch people's noses. He married the teacher of Class 2 in the boys' school. They went to live in the last house on the left from us, before the Picket Harp.

Another Mr Hodges was a teacher at the school. He lived in one of the first houses on the left in Hampton Street. We called him Mr Tadpole because his head had grown. He had to take his chaps to gardening and he reckoned to know about it but he knew no more than a bull's foot. He thought parsnips grew on trees. Dick Dyer was one of his cronies. If his stuff didn't grow Mr Tadpole would give him some more seeds.

Mr Hodges had an invalid wife, and I don't think she always fed him. One boy was sent up every day from school to Hodges' shop in West Street for 'a threepenny packet of biscuits for Mr Hodges' (the teacher was no relation) for his lunch. He came to Tetbury every day from Shipton Moyne, but he was originally a Tetbury boy.

One thing I remember, that big boat the Titanic, going down. But later, there was one more thing, about the war, and what I thought about it was that all boys were the same: the master read out the names of all the men on a troopship that went down; and he said 'That ship was so big it was reaching from the church down to the school.' It really worried me, and it puzzled me. I wished they wouldn't say such things.

Another thing in the war - there was a young man from Westonbirt, Tim Brown, who got killed: he was a real good cricketer, and he used to teach cricket to the boys. He was really professional. I was very sad when I heard that.

There were three schools, really, all separate from each other - you had to go outside one school to get to another. The infants' school was on the right; the boys' school was in the middle, with the bell; the girls' school was on the left, at the top of Cutwell Hill. There were three separate playgrounds too, but the infants went in through the boys' playground. So you didn't see any girls when you were in the boys' school.

Miss Goodrich, who used to keep the greengrocer's shop by the Town Hall, she was the girls' school teacher at that time. She had a son who was ill. All my sisters disagreed with her when they were at school, and I think others did too. She was miserable. She was a horrid teacher, known for it.

Those naughty boys used to be mad after girls, always trying to get in the girls' school after them. Jack Hayes from Upton was one of them. His father was the bailiff there and his mother was the lady who sold eggs, thirteen for a dozen. I used to fight his battles because he was a soft lad, but he liked girls! I used to fight for the street, too - mainly against Bert Bignell who was older than me. But Jack was more of a courting boy, pestering the girls - but they liked it, of course they did. I didn't care for girls then or later. I thought I would never get married. Then I was given this girl - but that's another story.

Outside the school, on the Knap, there were two features. One was a pump in the middle for water. It is still there but even in my day it hadn't been used for years. It didn't work because the water in the well underneath had become contaminated and they stopped it. The other thing was a very huge telegraph pole. The thing to do when you were in the boys' school was to climb right to the top of the pole. Well, I was very good at that - going up it. I was the best. I was the school champion at doing it in my time.

When I was at school there were several boys who came from Westonbirt. They all lived on a farm that belonged to the Westonbirt estate. They always brought their food for the day with them, and it was always the same - bread and butter, nothing else. They churned butter every day on the estate, and they always had lots of it, and apart from that they only had bread, so they had bread and butter. At dinner time people who didn't go home would open their sandwiches and the Westonbirt boys would try to swap what they had for something someone else had. Sometimes they managed to do it, but mostly they had to eat bread and butter.

I went to school like everybody else, but I didn't get much of an education because I was always tired. I always had to have a job to bring some money in.

There isn't a school there at all now.

There used to be a hooter at Cook's brewery that went at 6 o'clock in the morning and again 6 o'clock at night. My dad used to go to work by the hooter, every morning. But he wasn't the only one. My mother used to get me out of bed and, for several years, every morning I went to The Grey House in Hampton Street, cleaning boots, polishing knives and forks, getting coal out of the cellar and cutting faggots of wood and that, first thing. I worked at The Grey House for the Gippses.

Mrs Gipps was a lady, and at one time my sister Rene was a lady's maid to her. Mrs Gipps was Miss Golightly the Canon's daughter - he was the rector of Shipton Moyne - and she married Cyril Gipps (there's a story about Canon Golightly and my father, but that's a story about Shipton Moyne). The Grey House was in Hampton Street near the Register Office, opposite the big garage in Hampton Street, coming up from the corner of Chavenage Lane. I think this job started before I was twelve; they paid my mother three shillings and sixpence a week for the work I did. I didn't see any of it.

And then, when I had done everything at The Grey House I went to Milwards in Church Street to clean the shop. Milwards was a boot and shoe shop. It belonged to Bert Wheeler and Nelly his wife. While they were working they would always sing this song:

> 'Going along the road
> Perhaps you'll think me strange
> I lost me tripe and onions and
> Me fourpence ha'penny change.'

When the bell rang just before nine o' clock I went off up to school. Well, I got to school like that, while it was ringing. I ran down West Street. When I came out of morning school I went back to Milwards and I worked a session there; it was still open at twelve, and when they did close the shop at one o'clock, and everyone went to dinner, then of course I would go home.

I would go all the way home and all the way back, by running, and have my bit of food and always come back with a belt full of apples. We had a lot of apples. I never went out without apples. I wore a blouse, with strings, and the apples tucked in lovely in there. The other boys did it as well. I used to have a good binge.

Mr E T Lamb took this photograph of Church Street. He was Persis Lamb's father. His shop was on the left where the Perth Dyers sign is; the Eight Bells, where Eddie spent a lot of his time, is on the right.

I went right back to work again at Milwards after I came from school at 4 o' clock in the afternoon until tea time. I used to paint boots then, you see. They used to come in rough - heavy boots - and I used to paint them black, and all that kind of thing. There was always plenty to do.

Milwards had a proper cobbler called Mr Britton. He made shoes for Warns, the brewers. Warns were very great big people, size twelves and over. Mr Britton was quite old and he was marrying a woman from the Post Office. He got himself elated and made a lot of mistakes when he was hammering nails into shoes.

It was a wonderful job. I would do anything that I had to do. Clean it up. I often had to go up to the cobbler's part, and I used to watch him. That's how I got to mend shoes. That's how people learn - get enough graft to use the tools! My father used to do iron things and I know how to bang metal into shape. You can't help it.

This café used to be Milwards shoe and boot shop, where I worked before and after school. I always ask them about the speaking tube when I go in for a coffee, but they haven't found it yet.

The last time I went there (it's a café now) I went into the shop, and I said to the woman, 'Where's the speaker from upstairs?'

She said, 'There isn't one!'

I said 'There's one somewhere, you know!' It was a tube that went from the shop right up to the top where Mr Britton used to make the shoes. It was quite handy, because they were making shoes upstairs and had the shop downstairs. I reckon the speaking tube is still there somewhere, but they didn't know where it was!

There's a story: my Dad had a pair of shoes that wanted mending. They weren't his shoes at first, they were second hand; he got them from Jimmy Clark at the top of Long Street, on the corner. I took the shoes to be mended, with a five shilling piece (we called them cartwheels) to pay for them; but the main interest of the Wheelers wasn't boots and shoes, it was gobbling money, and Mrs Wheeler sent a second bill for the shoes. You would have thought they would have known it had been paid, because I worked there. There can't have been any problem. They only asked for the money again.

I used to go errands for the assistant at the counter, Isabel Parsons from Cutwell, for things like sweets, and I always thought she took the money for the sweets from the till. But I don't know, and I may have been wrong.

I went home after I had finished at Milwards, for my tea. The rest of the day, when there was no gardening or fetching water from Tetbury for drinking, I had to myself. It meant I never had any schooling. You know what I mean. You couldn't, could you? I was too busy. I began work at six o'clock in the morning, see. I missed out on reading because I was always busy, and usually at work. Mind you, I enjoyed work.

On Friday evening I had another job: I went to Wrights, the printers, the paper shop in Long Street. I used to go all round Tetbury to deliver the Wilts and Gloster Standard, but my main area was Charlton Road. When I got to the last house in Charlton Road there was still the pub, the Three Cocks. The Witchells were the farmers there, but the people who ran the pub were the Drissells. Between the last house and the Three Cocks I always used to sing 'Wedding Bells' in time to my feet as I ran there and back up the road to complete my round.

There's another story about Wright's shop: one week I fell ill and I missed a session. When I went for my money they gave me, not one shilling and sixpence, which was the wages for cleaning the shop and working Saturdays as well, but sixpence - yes, six pence - for the part time I worked. I went home and told my mother. She would get incensed over anything like that. She took it to the shop and gave them their own sixpence back. I don't know what she said to them. Well, I do, but I won't say anything about what she told them.

Oxford House was Pegler's shop, and the bakehouse, where I worked for years, was behind the right hand door. It is in Long Street opposite Gale's shop. It was a grocer's before Mr Pegler had it and it always had the split door.

Eventually I went to work for Gale's shop, the grocers in Long Street, as an errand boy, and then for Jim Pegler at his bakehouse opposite instead.

Now this is a roundabout story, but it proves I didn't have the worst life: a few years ago I was at Castle Coombe, what they call the prettiest village in Wiltshire - it's where I went first with Edith and my mother in the Morris Cowley I borrowed from Jack Clark (I paid him about what it

This picture was taken the first time Edith and I went to Castle Coombe. We went in the car Jack Clark hired to me for three pounds.

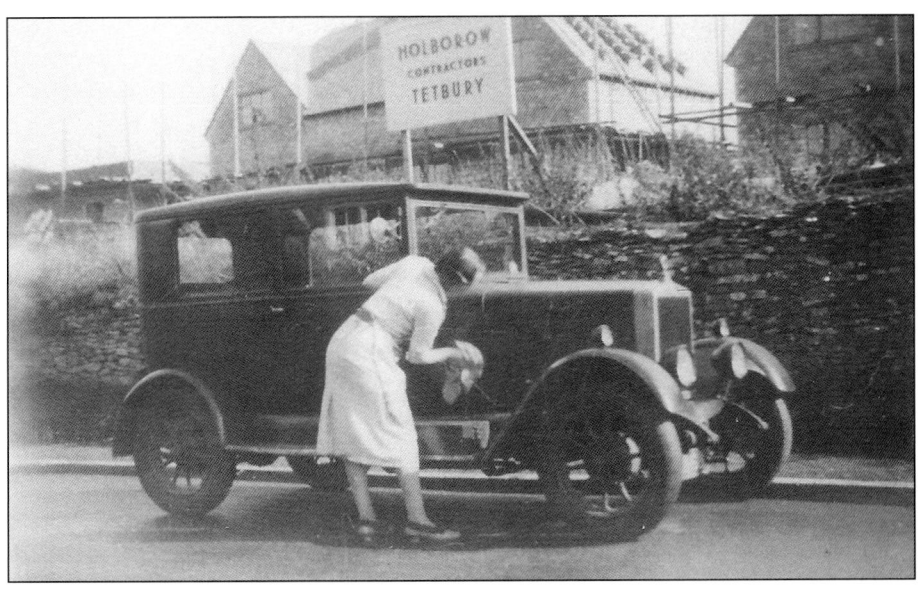

This picture is rare and historic. First, it shows the council houses being built by Holborow's in Coronation Road; second, it shows Edith polishing the car. That's a naughty thing to say.

was worth to borrow it for a few days - three pounds - I think he paid five for it - he was one of my Exclusive Brethren bosses and two of his sisters married my Vizor cousins). I got in the café and the lady said to me 'Where do you come from?' and I said 'Yes?' and I thought myself, What does she want to know that for? Because I thought I wanted to muddle her up a little bit, I said, 'From Yorkshire.'

She said, 'That isn't where your home is!'

'Oh yes,' I said, 'I live there.' She didn't mean that, she meant my native place. So I told her. I said 'Tetbury.'

'Why, I thought it was! You know, my husband's from Tetbury!'

I know all his family. The name is Constable, and they used to live half way down Cutwell Hill.

Anyrate, when I was about eighteen and working for Pegler I used to go round Tetbury with the bread, with the hand van, and I got talking with Mr Constable at Cutwell who was my Constable's great granddad, I expect he was. He was a real old man, he said he was about ninety years old then, and he would sit outside his house and talk to people. He said he knew the climbing boys well that went up the chimneys, to sweep the chimneys, when he was a boy. He wasn't joking - he told it to me as a real story and I believed him.

You used to be able to leave school at a certain age and go to work, but you had to get a certificate from the Head Master (Mr Webb at the time) to say that you had completed your education.

When it came time for me to have my certificate he wouldn't give me one because I hadn't got enough knowledge and couldn't read and write well enough! Of course, this was because I was always doing two jobs as well as going to school, so it wasn't surprising that I wasn't up to scratch. He made me stay on to the end of the next year, but at least I didn't have any problems with reading or writing by then. But I never got the habit of reading while I was at school, and I was always working such long hours after I left school that I never got the habit later on, though many's the time I wished I had.

I think I never got any chance to read, or anything. Anyrate, I would rather do a job, even darn socks, than read. But I do read now.

– THE FIFTH PART –

Family Matters

*N*obody gets their own food now, but all the men in Tetbury did it in that day, growing their own food. I used to have a garden at Kew Gardens, down by the railway. It used to be my Dad's and then it was mine, and that was for growing food, but he got an allotment up at Twelve Acres - go up Bath Road and turn right after the bridge, when you get up by Charlie Brown's funny looking house that was a toll house, right and then left - and he used to cut across the field from there after he left work at Witchells. He had the loan of the allotment from Witchell. I used to take him a can of tea there from home and he would work and work.

I remember Dad coming home and putting his wages on the table for Mother. He used to get paid, when I remember it, thirty shillings at the end of Saturday for a week's work to keep the whole family - the whole house. You couldn't buy meat or anything on thirty shillings, and you had to grow everything and go gleaning and keep a pig. We never had any money for food, but Dad grew most of it. When we had the two houses and the rent was two and six a week each, we paid five shillings. You have to remember that everyone was in the same state or worse. There were other young men in Tetbury who hadn't a cent and didn't know where the food was coming from. At that time Mr Medcroft's wages had gone up to eighteen shillings as a shepherd.

We had terriers and setters. Father used to breed them, and he used them to make friends. There was a fox-terrier at Wisteria called Gyp that was the father of the fox-terrier pups, and the bitch was Dad's, Nellie. Dad only sold them as puppies, but he was well known for it and people came from a long way off to buy a dog - a short haired fox-terrier. Flossie and Jessie were Nellie's pups, but there were more. Nellie was good for rabbits. We used to go up Blind Lane with her on Sunday.

The first time I went out poaching with Nellie, the first rabbit I got, I banged it on the head. I banged its head on the stone wall and it was dead, I thought. I was preparing my trousers, opening them up for putting it down them (in case I was seen carrying it). It was important to hide the rabbit, you see, because it was poaching, stealing the rabbit, and in particular, it was Sunday! I thought I had prepared for it, but the jolly rabbit jumped up and it ran away. But Nellie sprang at it and got it again straight away. She was as sharp as a needle.

Mother went shopping on Saturday. When I was very small I used to go with her, and later on I always went with her if I could. In those days you had to go to different shops - butcher, baker, grocer - even that was divided into groceries and provisions, which was cheese and bacon - and most things were loose, such as tea, butter and sugar: they put a paper on the scales and weighed out however much you wanted and then wrapped it up. One thing Gale's sold was butter colouring for the farmers and such who made their own butter. That's something you never see in a shop now! When it came to the cheese the assistant always said 'Would you like to taste it?' and Mother would lift up her veil - most women wore a veil then - and they would give her a small piece of cheese to eat, from the very big piece, the whole cheese, on the counter. The cheese was always covered with a kind of cloth. It was made like that. When she paid she would get a few sweets from them - they gave them to her - 'for the children'.

My Dad was in the Volunteers. He kept his rifle at home. It was in the cupboard under the stairs. It was as heavy as lead, as much as I could ever lift. The rifle stayed there until it was rusty, and after Mother died they took it away.

The Volunteers drilled all over the place in Tetbury, but they dug trenches, real trenches, for practice, in case they were wanted in the war. That was on the hill up past Cutwell. They used to dig their trenches in the field looking down on the left as you go down the hill from Cox's house to Cutwell. That's where they used to do it.

Every Saturday during the war Dad used to go down to Quedgeley to guard the ammunition. There was a depot there. Several men went from Tetbury together, in a car. But he was in the Volunteers before the war.

Dad smoked a pipe, and apart from the food he grew in the garden, he used to grow his own tobacco. He used to hang the leaves up to dry in a lean-to shed behind the house. It was a complicated business. He had a friend who was a gardener and he got this friend to germinate the seed for him. Everything else he did himself. He did the lot. He made all his own equipment. He made two presses, with a screw and a straight handle across, between two squares of metal, all made of steel, to put the tobacco in. He made the steel squares himself. He used to put stuff in to cure it, liquors and stuff - I know he used saltpetre, but he used rum, too. He used to press it every day. It was very clever. The last thing was bed-ticking. He made the tobacco into a packet with that and pressed down again. It was put down in layers.

Arthur Peters, my Dad, in his gardening hat. He worked every day but Sunday in the garden and on his allotment. This picture was taken in the garden at Upton Road. He grew most of our food, and a lot of tobacco as well.

When he had finished with it in the presses he would cut it very fine. He had a sort of machine, a cutter that he chopped the tobacco with, something like the machine a printer has for cutting paper, with a big knife that comes down, you know. And when he took hold of it in his hands, then it was tobacco. He made that machine himself, too. He used to keep the things in his garden shed, and he did everything he could do out of doors, in the garden, or set up behind the house in his lean-to, but when it came to the pressing and cutting he brought the equipment and the tobacco in the house and did everything there.

When I was a little boy I used to come behind him when he was sitting in his chair reading the newspaper and smoking his pipe, and the curlers came up all round him, and I enjoyed it! It turned out some good stuff. Dad brought it out at Christmas when it was seasoned and gave it to his mates as a present. I tried it myself once or twice, and it was all right, but I always preferred cigarettes to a pipe.

A Buffaloes' event in Malmesbury. I can't remember everybody's names now. Dad is ninth from the left, in his bowler. Mr Gething from the top of Long Street is wearing a cap, and Fishy Williams is next to him, wearing his apron.

He was in the RAOB, the Buffaloes - you know the meaning, the Royal Antediluvian Order of Buffaloes - and there is a picture of him with the rest of them in their bowler hats. It was supposed to be a club for charity, and it was, but mainly it was a boozing gang, though it wasn't supposed to be. We had his regalia in the house. There were a shield and stuff. They used to march in the procession at Tetbury Carnival. When there was any collection for charity they had everyone out as collectors. They had a bag on a long stick so that if anyone was in the bedroom when they called they could put the money straight in.

He always told this story against himself: they used to hold a lot of auctions in the Market House itself, during the day, and as he was working just across the road, where Troopers Court is now, he often would wander across to look around and see what was going on. He didn't mean to buy anything. There wasn't a lot of entertainment in those days. Sometimes he went and met some of his pals there, and one day they were all chatting while the auctioneer was going on. While Dad was talking he was waving his hands about and he heard the auctioneer say 'Sold to Mr AJ Peters'! He wasn't taking any notice of what was going on. Anyrate, he found it was two chairs he had bought, and he had to pay for them and take them away. He didn't want them at all, and I've no idea what happened to them.

Dad had a sense of humour and he liked a lot of the old songs and would sing them. He had a particular joke that he liked to play on people: he would bring out a small sheet of brown paper and say to somebody 'I want to show you a trick. Will you fold this piece of paper in half for me? Yes, like that. Now fold it again' - and so on. When it was folded as much as it could be he would take it from them and open it up and screw it into a ball and then ask them to scrumple it up as hard as they could. Then he would take it from them and open it again, and then do the whole business over again - folding, it, opening it, screwing it into a ball and scrumpling it again, and then he would take it from them, open it up carefully, examine it closely and then he would say, 'Yes, that's about soft enough. Thank you. Now I can go to the lavatory!'

Mother used to do most of her work in the living room, usually sitting at the table, and she always made a cake at the weekend before she went out to do her shopping, and she left Dad to bake the cake. Now there wasn't a proper oven, only one that he had made himself that sat in front of the fire. In fact he had to keep on making them. They were a sort of box made of thin sheet metal, and you had to keep them close to the fire and let them get hot. When he had got the cake in the oven he had to hold it in front of the fire and keep moving it so that the cake would get hot and bake. It took him all afternoon, and the cake wasn't well baked even then, ever.

When I got older and I was working at Peglers I sometimes took the cake to work with me and put it in the bakehouse oven with the rest of them - after it had been baked at home in Dad's oven and when it was finished - and when I took it out with the others it was just right. I had to put it separately from the others though, on a rack, and the cat got it every time!

Mother and Dad had their birthday together - his was 3 February and hers was 6 February. One year when I was a baker I sent them a birthday cake when it was their birthday. It was a proper decorated cake, and I packed it in a wooden margarine box with two nails driven into it from underneath to stop it sliding about. They didn't thank me because I never told them who sent it.

My mother loved me exceedingly. When I was working, if anyone gave me anything I would bring it home for her. I would take her shopping and tell her what to buy.

I think this is the last picture of Mother and Dad before he died in 1938

I'll tell you a story about Mother, and I wasn't there at the time, I only heard about it afterwards. Some crows had been pulling potatoes out from a truck, and some of our family found some that had fallen on the ground, and they took them home, quite pleased. Mother said, 'Take these back at once!' When I heard that, I knew then what she was like.

MY SISTERS

Vera was my eldest sister. It seems funny saying this, but she always ate dandelions, the leaves, you know, as a salad. She was often away, in service. Mostly it was the girls who were in service: they had a box of clothes from the school when they left to go into service. Vera had one, but Olive didn't get any clothes because she was going to work in Harvey's the grocer's shop; Rene didn't get any because she wasn't in Tetbury when she left school.

At first Vera was a housemaid at Gatcombe Park, and then she had the same job at 8 Thurloe Square in London. She would go away just like that. She was usually in service, but during the first world war, Vera worked for Harvey's, running the café that belonged to them next door to the Stores in Church Street. Vera kept the café and Olive worked in Harvey's Stores. That was when the Australians were based in Tetbury, and all the Australians came into the café and that's where both my sisters looked after them. There was one fellow Vera looked after, one of the Australians, who was higher in rank than the others, but all the time she was in love with her cousin Cuthbert Pike from Malmesbury. There must have been correspondence going on because by this time Bert was living in New Zealand, and so was his brother Ebby (Ebenezer).

Elgin House at the corner of Coombers Mead had lattice windows, and it was backed by the combing house. During the first world war the Australians lived there. I went in there once and over the fireplace it said 'Dinkum dinkum dinkum die'. I think it means something to do with 'true' or 'truth'. Leslie Purdue was one of them, an Australian who courted Olive for a long time, but then she married Fred Hills.

There was another Australian who owned a transport garage in Australia, and his name was Frank. He once gave me a pound because my name was Frank. He was a decent fellow. They were packed with money, not like our men. They used to spend money on kids. They liked to see kids fighting. I got a penny or something for fighting Bert Bignell.

When they were ready for marching, though, you never saw such a crooked lot of fellows! They would come out from where they were eating, form fours, and then straggle off like loose people.

When they finally left Tetbury they painted the animal, the sign of the White Hart, red white and blue; they poured petrol down the gutters and set fire to it; and they wrote all over the shop windows with soap. There was one accident: they used to use tenders, big motor cars like a lorry with seats, and when they drove away from Tetbury they were all having a jolly good time. They tore off, and a boy got caught on a tender and was carried away, hanging on the back. He was injured. I don't remember whether he died. But it was an accident. Leslie Purdue was in that tender.

They had lots of money and kept giving it away to children. I expect they were more normal and decent in their own country.

I remember, when Vera went away to New Zealand, my mother making little bags of cloth for her to wear down the front of her clothes, to put her money in, in case anything happened. Then, if they wanted to take her money, they would have to take her! But nothing happened.

Vera was like Mother, and as she got older she looked more like her. I wish she could have come home again, but she never came back from New Zealand. She was very unlucky with her boy dying and then her grandchildren drowning. I don't suppose she ever got over it. But part of her character was selfishness. Vera was always going out and changing her job, and because she was the eldest she always had the most money. Because she was working and had the money she used to buy herself things to eat that the rest of us never had. I remember her with a bar of chocolate. I think Laura to this very day has a grudge against Vera: Laura remembers once when Clarence was very little she saw Vera eating chocolate in front of him, and ignoring him, and she didn't give him any, though he was asking her for a piece all the time. There was always something a bit selfish about Vera.

Except for that short time in the war, Vera was always a servant. I think her first job was at Gatcombe Park, where the Princess Royal lives now; another place was Keevils, the farmer at Upton. She was usually looking after children; she worked for Keevil as a housemaid; she said they gave her all old food warmed up. I think she was the dishwasher there.

My sister Olive - Olive Alice - was lovely. At one time Olive worked for Pegler, in the shop in Long Street and for a long time at Harvey's Stores in Long Street. She always worked in shops and of course at last she had her own shop at Long Newnton Post Office: OA Hills. She used to sell everything there, including beer. The lorry used to come there from Devizes, from Wadworth's Brewery. It was all bottled beer. She had her own shop then, but she still helped people.

There were no girls like my sisters, especially Olive. That was my impression. Olive was the second one and she was a good girl all her life. She was always very good with the children and she would take them over from Mother. I sometimes still say 'Alice', because that was her other name: Olive Alice. I loved her more than anyone.

Olive told me, 'When you hear a pigeon, it's saying "My foot hurts, Bessie, my foot hurts"!'

Once when some people at Minety went away for a holiday she went and served in their shop and kept it open for them, and I took her there.

That was when I had a car, the air-cooled Rover Eight. It was like a cradle.

There was a man who was a professional shoemaker. He was courting Olive. His wife had died. When he was talking to Olive he was so excited he made mistakes in what he was saying.

Later she went to Cheltenham for a job at Melias. Then she married Fred Hills who worked for Holborows and they went to live at Long Newnton. A few years later they had the Post Office there until they retired.

Rene - Irene - came next, but for a lot of the time she wasn't at home because she lived with my uncle and aunt at the Waggon and Horses at Chedworth. That was Mr and Mrs Vizor - Uncle Alfred, my mother's brother, and Aunt Elizabeth. They had no children of their own.

Rene went to Chedworth School, but all the rest of us went to Tetbury National School. When she got a bit older she sometimes worked behind the bar at the Waggon and Horses, and after she came back home she worked for a while as a relief barmaid at the Talbot, and then as lady's maid for Mrs Gipps at The Grey House in Hampton Street. She married Billy Lewis, a butler, from Dolgellau in Wales, before I went to Hull. They went to a place near London to have a café. It seemed all right when I went there and stayed with them a little while. Billy got a job at Dursley and they came back to Tetbury and they took on number 4 Upton Road. Later they moved to Magdalen Villa in London Road.

I expect you have to have a proper way of talking to men if you're a barmaid, to keep them in order, and I think Rene could do that. She always talked to Billy quite sharply as if she was keeping him in order! We didn't get on very well when we were young but when she was older she was more sensible.

By the way, I went into a pub on the south coast once and the landlord was the last owner of the Talbot, Mr Eddels!

Once at work I was ill, and Mr Pegler wanted me to do some extra work, but when he saw what I was was like he said 'Get along home, have a bobsworth of brandy and go to bed!' Well, I paid the pub a shilling, got the brandy, and went home and came through the door and drank the brandy. It was a big cup full, like the mug I drink my tea from; I wasn't used to it, and when I went to bed I started to fall on to the floor. Rene was there and she caught me and put me back to bed. When I woke up I was better.

Laura was younger than me, and she went into service, looking after children. She was always looking after other people's children, even when she was quite young. When she left school she got a job with the Huntleys who lived at Boxwell Court, where eighty trees fell in the ferocious storm, when a tree fell across the road at Hunters Hall. The men who were working there at the back of the building came round to see what had happened and the roof slid to the ground behind them.

Mr Huntley was the proprietor of a brewery. Laura worked there as an under-nurse. It's near Kingscote crossroads. You turn left after one and a half miles. It's easy to find by the big white gates. Inside the gates there used to be thousands of rabbits. There was a marvellous very big pond with fish in.

She worked at Upton House, too, for Lady Guendolene, as nursemaid to the children.

Later she got a job in Derbyshire, and that was where she met Maurice Heathcote who worked as a chauffeur next door. She married Maurice and they went to live at Quarndon, just outside Derby. That's how you used to get people marrying who came from different parts of the country. One or both of them would be in service and they went to live where one or the other came from, or where the man got a job.

When Maurice married Laura, they didn't have a penny, and of course they didn't have a car, although he was a chauffeur. But his sister's husband gave them one that had belonged to them, quite an old one, and it was parked outside our house in the street. Clarence was a bit funny about it - I would say he was disparaging. When they drove off in Maurice's car I said to Clarence 'You look as if you disapproved.' He said, 'No, I'm jealous!' You know, neither Laura nor Maurice had two ha'pennies for a penny - they had nothing, and someone gave them a car. And Clarence was jealous!

MY BROTHERS

Eddie was always called Eddie, though his name was Edmund. I never chummed up with him and had very little to do with him when we were boys, unless it was tree climbing. We did that together. I got on all right with him.

Dad often called him Teddie, or 'our Ted', and he called him all sorts of other names as well, in a friendly way. If Dad didn't call me Frank he sometimes called me Frankie, but I thought there was a difference in the way he meant it, as if he was jealous of me. Sometimes he called me 'Mother's Frank'. But Dad was usually all right, and we got on. There was one day though, I was at the back of the house and I heard '...Frankie....'. It was Dad in the garden, and he was talking across to the Prices, and he was running me down.

I called out, 'Dad! Can you come in half a minute?'

He came in, and I put him right about it, and that was the end.

Eddie never had a proper job until he was much older, though you could often find him at Pegler's garage in London Road, working on a car. But they wouldn't want to pay him wages. He drove their taxi for them, but that wasn't all the time. He would go anywhere on his bike (or my bike) to earn something, doing odd jobs. If there was any beer about he would like it. That's what he was, an odd job man. Once I went with him to Badminton, to help with charging for the chairs for a polo match. All the toffs came along and Eddie was shouting 'Plenty of seats here!' He gave one of them the wrong change for a chair, but the toff said 'Oh, keep it!' Anyrate, it was Eddie's job, but they paid both of us.

Eddie thought a lot about girls. He spent a lot of time in the pub, mostly the Ormond's Head or the Eight Bells. According to my sister Laura, when he was in the army they called him 'Eddie the Red' - he was a barrack room lawyer. He was a friend of my dad and he was like him. I always thought, he was just like Dad might have been.

Raymond was my pal. He first told me in confidence that he had some money. He had saved five pounds. He was always very careful. I said 'You're doing the right thing!' and I gave him five shillings to put to it. He always saved. When he started work he would always be well dressed. He had a suit made with his name in it when he was quite young, about

20, and he kept it and wore it until he died. And he had a new pair of boots with very wide laces, his best ones. Every day when he took the boots off he would take the laces out and roll them up neatly. I told you, he was very careful!

Raymond worked for the butcher in Church Street, but when he left school he got a job with Mr Gale at the grocer's shop in Long Street, that used to be the Tetbury Stores once, and may have been an inn before that. Then he went to work for Mr Herring at Bicester, a big shop where there were twelve men assistants. Mr Herring was married to Charles Hedge's wife's sister. After Raymond left there, he went to a place in Wiltshire - Trowbridge. That's where he met his wife. He used to come home on the bus to see Mother, and when I was married and living at Bath Bridge he used to come and see us, too. He never forsook us. He was always one of the family.

When my brother Raymond owned the shop he did not change the name. Some people thought he was Mr Gale.

Of course, in time he and his wife bought Gale's shop, when George Gale retired and went to live in Devon. The shop worked after that. He used to oblige people. He ran long accounts, up to a year before he was paid, sometimes. Every one of his regular customers had a book, and he wrote down every transaction. A lot of people paid once a week or once a month. But he knew how to charge to make up for it! Everything was a penny or twopence more. I was quite startled once when I saw what he was charging for toilet rolls!

You know, in the later years, a lot of people thought he was Mr Gale!

Clarence was the baby of the family. When he was a boy he was tiny. Once I was poorly in bed and he came into bed with me and tickled me with his eyelashes.

Clarence was always the same towards the family as Raymond, except when he got a job with the solicitors in Tetbury and got on a bit. He would be walking down Long Street in his suit, and he wouldn't see me. You see, I was with the baker's barrow, taking it round town, and he was dressed up. And he always had money then, and I hadn't. And he had always had money, because he was the baby.

Mother and Dad, me on the right, Raymond in the middle, Clarence and Eddie in front, I can't remember exactly, but it must have been taken in 1937 on my last visit home before I married Edith.

Later he worked for Satteleys the jeweller (one of his jobs was to wind the church clock) and then he worked as a jeweller in the Midlands and later bought a shop in Hull. He was an instrument technician LAC in the Air Force in the war - one of his jobs was on that bouncing bomb - and he said he learned more as a tradesman from the training courses he went on in the RAF than all the time he was at Satteleys and all the rest of his job.

When he was courting his wife he said to me 'She's nothing like our sisters and they're nothing like her.' Well, that's what he said. But I always thought my sisters were wonderful.

He was quite young and innocent when I brought Edith home with me to stay. He got a tall ladder and propped it up against the wall outside her bedroom so that he could talk to her through the window.

– THE SIXTH PART –

My Career

PEGLER'S MAN

I worked for Peglers, the bakers, in Long Street, part-time when I was still at school and full-time after I left school, and then I left and got the job at Pellys, The Priory. If you want to know why I left, it was Mrs Pegler. I was sick to death of her. She had a pretty face but she was an awful hag. There was a window in the bakehouse and you could see in and on Monday morning you could see her doing her washing and grumbling all the time.

When I was earning some money (not much, because I was working for Mr Pegler) I went to the Lambs' studio in Church Street. Persis Lamb took this picture. It isn't in good condition because it was damaged in a flood of sewage while we were moving house early in the war.

And they got another man to do my job. I was at The Priory for a while but then I heard Peglers wanted a man. The fellow they'd got was no good at the job. At that time it was Mr Pegler, Jim Pegler, and his son Gilbert, who had been in the cavalry in South Africa. The other Pegler, Gilbert's brother Reg, went to be a baker at Cricklade. I've seen his notice from the delivery bike in the museum there.

Jim Pegler was originally a baker for Lewises. Ralph Cleaver was a baker there too, then. Mr Cook and Mr Caborn were working together there as well, and like Jim Pegler, they were in the Brethren.

I'm going to tell you a lie, now. I'm sorry, but I've made my peace with it, because it was a bare faced lie, was this one. They'd had the man at Pegler's and he was no good. Didn't know what he was doing. Anyrate, it came empty, the job, you see. I was still working at The Priory then and I went back to Pegler's for the job. Mr Pegler came through the door and stood up: 'Hello, Frank!'

'Well,' I says, 'I see you're in want of a man,' I says to Pegler.

He looked over his glasses at me and he sort of smiled to himself. 'Oho!' It was all glitter because he knew that he'd have had a fellow there that did what I had to do. I said what I said, and he said, 'You can have it.' Now he said, 'What about the money?'

'Well,' I said, 'I've been earning such a lot, a good bit now. Quite a bit; but I shouldn't come back - I wouldn't like to come back - for *that*.' Cause I didn't think that was enough. So I asked him for a bounce. That meant I was asking him for over a pound a week. Now wages were very bad then, but I should have asked for more than that. I think I was earning fifteen shillings a week at The Priory, and that was more than Pegler had paid me.

'You can have it!' he says. 'That's all right!' I ought to have asked for more. He didn't know, but I got a bounce. That was satisfactory, that. He took me on and paid me what I wanted - one pound five shillings, and only too glad to have me!

There was a follow-up to that: in those days you had a National Insurance card, and your boss had to put stamps on it. After I had left Pellys at The Priory I had my card to take to Pegler and get it stamped, but I had been looking at what it said on the card, and when I got paid I said to Mr Pegler 'What does this mean? "If your remuneration does not exceed thirty shillings a week, the employer has to pay it all".' It was something like that.

'I'll show the missus,' he said. Up to then I was paying my eightpence a week myself. Now it seemed money was coming in from all over the place: I had a pay rise and I had an extra eight pence!

I was very young then, and I thought it was a grand job. I went home one day and started making some big plate mince pies. My brothers really enjoyed them. We always enjoyed our life. People didn't have anything but they weren't miserable.

Soon this was what I did: everything. Not just baking bread. It started off with me working in the bakehouse baking from early morning, and then doing the town, delivering the bread all round Tetbury with the hand van. It was a proper baker's van, a hand drawn van that could go round the town. You didn't need a driver's licence! That was my last job of the day.

At first Jim Pegler had a horse-drawn van and the hand-van - you pushed it along. When Mr Pegler had his first bakehouse, in Church Street, Lizzie, Gilbert's wife, used to drive the horse van. It was a little horse-drawn van, about so high, with a curved roof, and she sat up on top, on the roof, to drive it. She drove it all through the first world war. They kept the horse in a field on the Westonbirt road. It was a job to catch it and bring it into Tetbury! Then he got a motor-van, and then a van and a car, and at last two vans.

Mr Pegler was one of the first tradesmen in Tetbury to have a motor van. That was after the first war when they moved to Long Street (their first bakehouse was next door to Phillips' in Church Street - it belonged to someone called Maggs before they had it). First they used to keep the van in a yard up at The Chipping, in a garage for motorbikes, and Gilbert Pegler drove it. When they were ready to take the bread out to the customers somebody had to go up there and bring it down to Oxford House in Long Street and park it there at the kerb. When we had finished the bread and it came out of the oven we brought it out of a door at the side and we stacked it on racks to cool. In the winter it was dark there, and a light was switched on every morning so that we could see what we were doing. Do you know, the first bulb in there, when they got electricity, one with a pip on it, an ordinary one - twenty-one years that lasted! Then we would bring the stuff out down the passage to Long Street and load the van. You couldn't do that now - there's too much traffic. Especially if Gale's had their van loading at the same time! We always loaded the van that way.

When we had two vans, we kept them in the yard up Hampton Street that belonged to the brewery.

When I put the hand van away in the garage up Hampton Street one day, it was when Gilbert Pegler was putting the motor van away, and he climbed up on the wall to watch the cricket. Well, I says meself, if he can, I can! So I got up on the wall with him and as long as he was watching the cricket I stayed up there too.

When Peglers first had the van, because of the war they couldn't get petrol. So they filled the tank with paraffin and used enough petrol to prime it and pushed it off down The Chipping (the road, not the steps). That got it going. Then they would keep the motor running all day, on paraffin.

I had a driving licence from 1931 to 1989, but it was years before I had a licence. At first I would go with Gilbert as his assistant, the driver's mate, and take the bread into the houses. But if he parked in a field, because some of our customers lived a long way from the road, he might go with the bread himself. Then he left me with the van, to 'look after it'. I would start it up and try the gears and drive a little bit in the field, and that was how I got started, really, to learn to drive. It was like trying with a bike. That's how you learn to ride a bike, isn't it? You try, don't you? Then I learned to drive across fields in Pegler's van, any time, with Gilbert Pegler. So it came natural somehow. But when I had some idea Gilbert Pegler took me up in his own car on to the Shipton Moyne road, which is a very narrow one, and taught me how to turn the car round. I had to turn round in front of a telegraph pole, but I did it. I got round.

It was a Citroen car I was driving but I couldn't have done much speed. Later, I was going up Fox Hill with him and I had to change gear because of course it didn't go fast, and I missed the gear. Gilbert caught hold of the gear handle and pulled it out of gear and we had to stop the thing. You didn't have to pass a driving test in those days. But of course, there was nothing about, was there? There was nothing about. Well, fancy!

Mind, I worked very hard - very hard. My brothers and sisters, the ones who were younger than me, said, 'We never know anything about Frank - he's always working!'

The point was, I used to get to work at Pegler's there, we'll say at four o' clock in the morning. When I finished baking at dinner time I went home to wash and get tidied up and come back.

Now as soon as he knew I could drive, when he knew he had a foolish fellow, Mr Pegler had me doing everything at the bakehouse until it was time to go home and then he would give me some driving to do, about twelve miles round. He would have his van ready with what he wanted me to go with and when I got back to the bakehouse he would say 'You wouldn't like to do a run for me, a little journey for me? Go up to where those animals are alive, look, those big animals?' He wanted me to do a delivery in the van. What do you call the animals? Brocks? The brocks were out by Culkerton, on the Ciren road. Well, I did a little round for him. If he wasn't ready I went for to get the van myself, from up by the street, or in the Chipping or up Hampton Street, at the brewery, and I'd get up and go off again, you see.

I would be there and come back again, and then I suppose I'd go off by myself afterward, and do what I was going to do, which was usually delivering bread round Northfield with the hand barrow. That was Pegler!

That was quite a job to do, but I used to do it, see? Anyrate when I got back home it was three o' clock, and the only thing wrong was that my mother used to be a bit vexed to think that I had been so long before I got back - anyrate that's what I was doing and twasn't spare time. No overtime. There's two sides to it, of course. I wanted to drive!

When I could drive Pegler's van by myself I would do all sorts of silly things. I would go down one hill as fast as I can and straight up the other side until I came to the farm gate and then BRRRRRRMMMM! straight into bottom gear and turn the van in at the gate.

When we had finished the day's journey we would count up all that was left and compare it with that day last week and cut it down or put it up. Once we made a mistake and made a batch of bread too many. We sold all that next day: it was only a day old!

There used to be one baker I knew had a secret recipe for putting an extra gallon of water in and he would get three extra loaves out of the mix. Pegler did things differently. He was a very good businessman in one way, because he controlled waste very carefully. People would come into his shop and ask 'Have you got a loaf of yesterday's bread, please?' and the answer was always 'No, sorry.'

You see every bag of flour was accounted for, and every loaf. Sometimes we would be one or two loaves short in the day, and the shop would sell out, but we never had any yesterday's bread! We never had any waste. He was good like that. There was never more than one or two loaves left over, and that was only sometimes, and when that happened, do you know what he did? He got a bucket of water, and if there was a loaf left from yesterday he dipped it in quickly and put it in the oven, with the next day's first batch of bread, and when it came out, why, it was new bread!

Talking about bread, of course I was a baker for years and years and I've made thousands of tons of bread in my time. There's no flavour to most modern bread, though I've just had a very expensive loaf called 'old-fashioned' that was very nice. I don't believe most supermarket bread is bread at all. They have a thing called White Hovis. We used to make Hovis bread, and it was special brown bread made in a tin marked Hovis, and if you made white bread dough and baked it in that tin you could get into trouble and be fined. Did you know that? And Hovis was special brown flour that had the extra wheatgerm that had been taken out of white flour.

We didn't make much Hovis, just one bag of flour at a time. We tipped into the bin and went on until we had used it up. Sometimes when you left it in the bin the Hovis flour came alive before you had used it all, and then you had to throw it away. But nowadays I think they just take all the wheatgerm out of it. I don't know what they do with it.

An old baker, Mr Topps, whose bakehouse and shop were by the Town Hall, once said to me after he retired, 'I don't know how these young men get up at two o' clock and go baking!'

I said 'What did you do? I used to go earlier because I had to put two faggots into the hot oven.' But that's another story, about Down Ampney. We all knew Mr Topps used to get up, himself, all his life at two o'clock and light the faggot that had been all night in the hot oven.

His wife was some relation to Mrs Pegler, I think. He lived to be a good age, and so did his father. I knew his father, too: he was a pig-sticker, used to kill and dress pigs.

Topps' shop became Stanley Marks after he retired.

When I worked for the Peglers we had an oven that you had to fire in the usual way and you put the loaves in during the afternoon to bake. It was a slow process, not like nowadays, but there was food in bread, and it had a wonderful taste. Peglers was a modern bakehouse for its time, with machinery, all run from belts coming down from the roof. But there used to be a lot of hard work in baking. You had to bring the flour down some steps from the loft where it was kept, and Mrs Pegler was always there, doing her own cooking in the kitchen which was next to the bakehouse and keeping her eye on us. At first we had to mix the flour and water by hand and leave it in the trough to rise. Afterwards we had a machine that stood against the wall that mixed the flour and water, but it was still a heavy job. You had to put two bags of flour into the machine, and when the dough came out you had to handle it and weigh it and stack it and put it on shelves to rise. But it was comparatively modern. Gilbert Pegler lived in the shop in Long Street at one time, and his wife - she was a nice person. But when the shop went, she lived in next door, where I've told you the postman and shoe mender, Corney Mann, had it. She may have been older than people thought.

Gilbert was only sixty when he died.

She was a Smith. The Smiths lived on the left of Cirencester Road, past the Oak. The old father lived in the big house and he had a lot of sons, and they all lived close together. When Gilbert got married they lived in the first house, and some of her brothers and Mrs Bond and Mrs Hayes (her sisters) all lived in the same row. Shortly after they got married she turned the tap on and couldn't turn it off and she ran home for her Dad.

This is the story that has to do with Holborow's greengrocer's shop and Gilbert Pegler. One day I was out in the country with Pegler's van, Kingscote way, and I saw a lot of rhubarb in a field. It just dawned on me because I knew the airfield wanted loads of rhubarb, to use it for pies, you know. I said to the fellow, 'Oh, what a lot of rhubarb!'

'Eeah, the stuff!' he says. 'Can't do anything with it! I don't know what I be going to do with that! It's been here for years, and if I had been like you....Tisn't worth picking.'

'Well,' I says, 'what about me offering you a penny a pound for it, then?'

'Well,' he says, 'you can have it!'

So I says, 'Well, I can't do that on my own, because I'm delivering bread.' So I went back down to Gilbert Pegler, because I was going on my way home. I thought he would come with me. And share, I suppose.

When I got back to Tetbury I told Gilbert about the rhubarb and he was agreeable and he says, 'All right, Frank, you slip now as quickly as you can and get cleaned up and changed, and get your tea, and we'll go back and get it.'

And I slipped and got some tea. I ran quickly enough because I was interested in it, and come back again. And he had been and got it all for himself. I'd been done! Right. That was Gilbert Pegler! Good firms, aren't they? Right oh.

So about the next day I went to Wiltshire way: Oaksey, Chelworth and Somerford Keynes and all round (you know, Oaksey was Mrs Medcroft's home - where she came from); and on the way back I saw another load, just the same as that. I think it was a distant relative, but I'm not sure; anyrate, top of Sunset Hill, just past Long Newnton. I says to him, 'Cor, what a lot of rhubarb you've got there! What are you going to do with it?'

The shop on the right is Holborow's greengrocers where I sold the rhubarb for 3d a pound.

'Aagh, a lot of stuff!' - you know. Grumbling.

'There's..... - I'll give you a penny a pound for it, then. If you like. Get rid of it somewhere.' And I got it.

On the way back to Pegler's I called at Holborow's with it. But when I got

120

down to Peglers I just calmly said to Gilbert 'Oh ho ho! Ah well, you didn't have that lot of rhubarb!'

He said 'What lot of rhubarb?'

I said, 'Well, I just brought in a load of rhubarb.' I got - I forget, no, threepence a pound. You see, twopence on a penny was worth it. I told him. I can't remember the end of it, but I thought it was awfully mean.

I always finished up doing more when I was working for Pegler. One thing that you don't even think of now is bags of flour - you just buy them in the supermarket. But when I started as a baker you bought your bag of flour from the baker. You had to pack flour (in your 'spare time') say at the end of the day, for customers to buy in the shop. Then someone would say 'You're useless! Leave it to Frank!' and I would be left with all the flour to pack while they finished.

When you were working in a bakehouse like Pegler's you never had a chance to get away from it or sit down. You were making dough, putting loaves into tins, twisting dough - when I had left baking and I was working in a factory people would say, 'Frank, come and sit down!' and I did, but I soon got up again because I wasn't used to it.

You know, people have said Mr Pegler used to go round and tell people what he thought of his workpeople: 'Real lot of good young people we were!' and then that's what he did. He didn't really appreciate us, he couldn't have done, could he?

Just being mean. Talk about being mean! Now, did you know the end of it? Well, you know when Easter come, don't you? Well, that ended up, Thursday night ended the work, didn't it? Of the bread and delivery and stuff? Well then, from then I never went home. I went on with the dough making, making Easter buns all night, and in the morning I took them round to the various people, in the van, that had ordered them, you see, and this is it: and I thought myself, well, he'll be touching me for something for doing this over all night. All night! And so he says when he pays me, he says: 'And that's for the helping with the buns - two shillings!' So I had a florin for the work. But he did give me a lift somewhere where there was a Brethren meeting that weekend - he was going to go there anyway.

Don't think I'm funny, but I think in his time he's done shifty shifts. I don't think that's done any good at all. I think you want to act fair with people, don't you? If you can possibly manage it. But that's it.

Jim Pegler, who was Gilbert's father, lived over the shop in Long Street with his first wife. I remember her well. She was very kind but very awful. She used to grumble and grumble, especially on a Monday morning. Mr Pegler would say 'Mother, Mother, please remember where you were yesterday.' Oh, he was a faithful man! Well, you can see! He had a number of ladies. There was one woman in Cirencester, and another, called Miss Long, in Cutwell. Miss Long had a son called Eddie: I think I know who the father was.

One day at work my mate Cyril Newman, who lived in the house opposite the shop, heard them rowing. The door was shut but he heard Jim Pegler and Miss Long (and they were having a going over) and she said: 'Jim, you promised to marry me!' But he married a Miss Selby as his second wife. She was an old maid, who was related to the Dolphin Coal and Coke Company. When he got married he moved into her house on the right hand side of Cirencester Road, past the Oak, almost opposite where Gilbert and Lizzie lived.

When I started in the van it was with Gilbert driving; later I went by myself, or I had someone with me who couldn't drive. We delivered bread all round Tetbury and the surrounding district, every day, and I used to have a long journey on Tuesday that started early and finished early - about three o'clock to three o'clock - and Gilbert's day was Friday.

By the way, that was after we had worked in the bakehouse from four o'clock in the morning making the bread and baking it. Sometimes we didn't get home until eight o'clock at night.

Mr Pegler had a car as well as the van - there were not many other cars about, were there? And the point of all of it is, what you did in cars then you wouldn't dare to be doing today, would you? Once when I went out with the van for him, out at Beverstone delivering bread, I had the front wheels went wrong. They were going opposite - you know, breakaway - and I thought, I can't turn it round. The wheels were turning out in opposite directions. I went home like that with the wheels all crooked. The axle - that was what had broken. You wouldn't dare to go like that now! Sometimes it would turn in like this and sometimes it would turn out like that and I took it straight to the garage in Hampton Street when I got it back to Tetbury, and walked back to Peglers to tell them. At least then there was nobody else about, was there?

Another thing I did was going out when you couldn't start the van - I used to let it run and then put it into gear and then it would start, you see? When you got going in that day cars weren't fast. They would do about thirty miles an hour. If you bought a new car it might even have the carburettor pinned down so that it wouldn't go any faster than that, if it was your first time with a car. But at least there weren't any other cars to run into!

Mr Pegler was all right as a driver. He once bought an Austin and it was always in the garage, up having something done to it. It was really a dud, if they don't know. You know the handles of the brake and gears? They were covered with lovely leather. He didn't use the clutch. I used to do that, too. I'll tell you what I mean: I was taught by Laura's husband, Maurice, he's a motor man, and he showed me how to do it, to change gear without the clutch. The point was, Mr Pegler never used the clutch to change gear.

At one time Gilbert Pegler had a three wheeler Morgan. He used to drive it fast, and it made such a noise that you could hear it going round Northfield when you were in Upton Road. Mind you, you could hear anything then! One day as he was driving it and I was in it with him the front wheel came off, but it stayed upright.

I don't think anyone was so foolish as Gilbert Pegler when he was driving. One day Gilbert and the farmer from Calcot Farm were coming into Tetbury from Calcot. The farmer had a car and Gilbert was in his van and they were racing each other down New Church Street, and going that fast! Coming out of New Church Street and turning right into Long Street up to the Town they both nearly went into the police station. That was in the good old days! He usually had a car, when he was young and when he was older, though at one time when his children were young Gilbert had a great big motorbike and sidecar. He used to take his whole family to Weston super Mare for the evening in summer, sitting one behind the other in the sidecar.

At first I delivered bread for Pegler all round Tetbury using the hand-van, and then I started delivering in the country, driving the van. But a bit later he started using a private car with a great big luggage grid on the back to do the Tetbury delivery, and that became my job, too.

One day I was delivering round the Knap with the car, in the ice, and I came round by the school at the top of Cutwell Hill, and I couldn't stop. I began to slide down the hill. Then I managed to lock the steering. I turned the car right round and began to go down backwards, on the tilt all the way. I got it over as far on the right as I could. I thought, The first thing it'll hit will be the house! and then it slid into the wall of a house and I got it stuck there. I left the car where it was and went down Charlton Road to Mr Hedges and he helped me to get it out.

There was a mark on the wall for years, a hole, but I think it has been put right now. People would think it's all lies, but it's simple sailing.

When we first had two vans I drove one and Gilbert had the other. That was when I did my journey round the farms and villages, from Bagpath up towards Uley, to a place called Symonds Hall Firs (except they always called it Zimmerzalvirs), and back through Leighterton. In the other direction I went to Ewen and Kemble and Culkerton. I called it 'my journey in the country'.

Well, after we all came back to live in Tetbury I had days when I had a journey in the country with a van, sometimes by myself, sometimes with Harold Major, sometimes with young Malcolm, and that was most of that day's work.

When the aerodrome at Kemble was first opened I saw all this great stretch of tarmac in front of me - they had lights like traffic lights that came on when a plane was coming, and you used to have to wait. It was the runway! I drove straight up this great road as fast as I could and a man came out from the tower to stop me. He stuttered when he spoke to me: 'IIIII cccould have you pppput in jail!' The man stammered: 'You don't know at what moment an aeroplane is coming down!'

Boys will be boys, as they say.

The two old vans were OK, but the new Bedford ones we had after the war, in 1946, were very poor. The mudguards were so thin and weak you could move them about with your hands, like a piece of paper. They were very poor. The rear wings were like bicycle mudguards. When it was wet the water poured off them. One of the men had to drive his van every morning through a place where water came out of the ground, and the water actually cut through it in a short time. But even when the vans were new you could waggle the wings with your hand.

The registration numbers of our new vans were 15 and 16. Gilbert asked me which one I would like - I could choose. I didn't like 15 for some reason, so Gilbert had that one and I had the other. He went off in his new van and something went wrong, I can't remember what, but it was something to do with the water.

When I was going round in the van I sometimes used to pick some flowers and take them home to my mother or later on my wife. Once I got some beautiful fritillaries from a place I knew at Oaksey, to take them to Edith. When I got back I met Gilbert, and I said 'Isn't that lovely?'

'What's lovely?' he said.

'These flowers!'

'Well, they're only flowers!'

Well, that was Gilbert Pegler! There's quite a lot of things involved in all this.

When Gilbert's boy Malcolm was five years old he went to school, and when he came home they asked him what he had learnt, and he told them they had done something about 'fairies at the bottom of the garden'. You wouldn't believe it, but Gilbert got in a frenzy about it. You see, he was a good man, but a bit religious, and he knew he didn't want his child taught that there were fairies, especially at the bottom of the garden.

'Why,' I said to him, 'they aren't really teaching him that there are fairies in your garden. It's to do with a child's imagination, bringing him on.' But he was difficult about it.

I had a customer in Cottons Lane, Mrs Prosser, who said to me when I was delivering bread, 'Let's see how many loaves I want today. I've got a stale bottom...' I haven't forgotten that!

Mrs Lewis lived at The Green. She was a fussy customer. One day she said, 'That's not a nice loaf,' as I was delivering it. She knew I had another one. I took it back outside and I threw it into the big basket. I put it in one side of the van (it was the one I pushed round Tetbury) and took it out from the other. Then it went back into my hand basket and I brought it back into the house. I said, 'I'm sorry, I gave you the wrong loaf.'

She liked that one. 'Why didn't you bring me that afirst?' she said.

Her husband was called Francis Lewis, and I don't know for certain but I think Mother had the idea of the name Francis for me from him.

One day I was delivering up our way, towards our cottages, with the hand van. It was so loaded that the back wheels were trying to come off the road, and it came on to rain. I should have covered the bread up before I set out, but I hadn't, and I knew I would get into a load of trouble if I got it wet. Do you know what I did? Well, nothing - I stood back, and I was on the edge of the rain. Everything in front of me was wet, and everything behind me was dry. I stayed where I was and the bread stayed dry.

My uncle worked on a farm at Bagpath. The person that rented it, that Edwin Cox worked for, got the push for having a dirty farm. I used to deliver to him and he didn't like paying. Once he kept me an hour, saying he was just going to pay me and hoping I would go away. But I had told Gilbert Pegler that I would get the money, and Gilbert was waiting for me. I waited for an hour. I waited and waited. And I got it.

There was another woman there in Bagpath who went on crutches, one of several who used to hope for their bread. She had a regular order, and when we were coming down the road she would go and hide in the wood until we had gone. One day she went upstairs to hide from me and Gilbert, but he knew where she was and he shouted 'Come on, Missus! I know you're upstairs!'

I used to deliver bread at Owlpen. There used to be two houses on the street corner opposite, and I used to deliver to one of them. Now they have both gone. You would never believe that there had been houses there. An old man lived in one of them, where you turn down to go to Horsley: he could always tell you what the weather was going to be, especially if it would rain.

I used to go in the other direction, starting at Long Newnton. I delivered to my sister Olive when she had the post office, and then to Brown's, and then I went on to Crudwell.

You know, bluebottles are horrible. They get on meat and spoil it I was in a house at Crudwell, nearly to Malmesbury, and the lady, Mrs Franks, wanted me to tell her where to cut the pig. The bluebottles had been at it. 'Bay-kah!' she said (that's how she always spoke to me), 'Bay-kah, what shall I do?' The pig was a wartime pig: it had two heads and eight legs, and a bit had gone bad. That was a lively job! I would have told her to cut it a bit further than she did, and give me some, but she didn't. She always paid me well, though - not just in money. One year she gave me a Russian duck for Christmas. Oh, it was wonderful! You cut and cut and you didn't get down to the bone! And, do you know, from other customers, I got two cockerels, and that's all we had for Christmas! That was just after the second war, when everything was rationed, even bread.

Once I was on my round, delivering bread in Crudwell, and I frightened a cockerel that did something I have never seen before or after. It ran from me and began to fly across a pond. But the pond was too long and the bird couldn't fly so far and landed on the water. And then it sort of ran over the surface until it reached the other side.

One day, when I was on my journey in the country, I was taking the bread to a farm, and I saw a fox get a chicken. I shouted, and it let go. When I saw her, I told the farmer's wife. She was pleased that the fox had missed the hen. Next time I came, she had the fox on a bench, peeled.

Another place where I delivered was a farm at Culkerton belonging to a big farmer called Mr Clark, a Christian. There was an old gentleman who lived opposite a row of farm cottages, in a bungalow, and he was the father of several of the workers. All the people that occupied the set of cottages were Mr Clark's workmen. I think the story was about a chopper, a billhook, that got stolen from one of the cottages when all the men were at work and all the women were at work. The door was left open, which was usual. At first they thought the billhook was probably stolen by the gipsies, though they knew they didn't usually steal things, only food.

A man had left the farm - he must have had some incentive - and the man who replaced him, a stranger, was the one who stole it. The old gentleman in the bungalow was offended by the shock - he couldn't believe that anyone who worked for Mr Clark could have walked into someone else's cottage and stolen anything. When this man stole the billhook (or whatever it was - I can't think what these people had to steal) that was the biggest news ever in Tetbury. The biggest thing there was.

And another thing - I was compelled to take marrows and cabbages and stuff home with me. Now, they would leave say a marrow on the table, or some onions, and if they met me they would say, 'Have these onions, Baker!' or 'Have the marrow!' Didn't we have some food! I would put the basket down on the table, and the vegetables would be there. 'Here, Baker, have some carrots!' I used to keep a great sack hanging up behind the pantry door, under the stairs, full of more vegetables than we could eat, sometimes.

In the war time, people had nothing; but in the country they had eggs. Now you know that as soon as he knew I could drive Pegler had me doing everything at the bakehouse until it was time to go home and then he would give me some driving to do, about twelve miles round.

I did exceedingly well one Christmas time. I always used to do well at Christmas, but this was exceptional. That day, the day of my last journey before Christmas, I was by myself and I got back to Peglers with five dozen eggs. You know, I used to do little things for them and they didn't have money - this was my Christmas tip! Some gave me a couple of eggs and some gave me more - half a dozen here and half a dozen there. When I got back to the van I put them in my flour basket to carry home, and when I was leaving Peglers I got my mac with the long pockets inside, over my smock that I wore, and put all the eggs into the pockets and went home to Bath Road. I don't know how I got back - all the way up Long Street and Church Street, and ever so relieved when I was on Bath Bridge and I could see our house!

Mother Metcalfe was there, staying with us, and when I got in I said, 'Oh, Grandma, look here!' and I brought two eggs out of my pocket. She loved eggs, and they were rationed. She was delighted. 'Oh, here's another couple!' I said, and so on, until all sixty eggs were on the table. She laughed all the time.

When I was driving the van for Pegler and I had Harold Major with me, I drove and he took the bread into the houses. He was a very nice man and he would hobnob with all the customers. When we got to Boxwell Court, the brewer's house, where Laura trained to be a nursemaid, Harold would go and hobnob with the boss while I waited for him in the van. The man would offer Harold a drink and Harold always accepted; and there I was, waiting for him outside, waiting to drive off. He was very quick, but he managed to get a drink every time the boss was at home and he met him. Wherever Harold Major was he would be in a pub. But when we called at Boxwell Court the boss always had him in for a drink.

Harold was a nice man, and he was a kind man, too. If he thought someone would like to have something of his he would give it them - anyone at all. I have seen him with a rabbit - he was always catching rabbits - and someone, anyone, I can't remember, said 'That's a nice rabbit you've got there!'

'Have it!' said Harold, and he gave it to them. That's the sort of man he was.

One day on my rounds I was at a farm and Harold Major was with me. We both had our baskets with us because we had to walk a long way from the van to deliver bread to the houses. As I was going along I saw a man bring a heavy horse out of the stable. He took it up to a barrel of water and it put its head down to drink. The man was standing right behind the horse, right against it. We were coming back with our empty baskets, and one of us, or both, did what we always did - slung the basket over our shoulder. That startled the horse. Then it made a noise, and it kicked out behind, and it hit him in the face with its hoof and down he went on the ground, such a mess! Harold and I were working and we couldn't stay. I don't even know if they took him to hospital, and I don't know now what happened to him after, but I came home and told everybody about it.

Another thing that happened was when Harold was delivering with me. There was an old lady who lived some way out of Crudwell village and she used to go there from her house on her bike. She was a nice lady, one of our customers. Harold watched her for a bit, and then he said 'Bet I can get her off her bike!' And he did. Harold was a bit naughty sometimes. Anyway, we thought afterwards, it could have killed her!

I used to know Mr Wills from the tobacco company: he lived with his daughter at Hunters Hall, and he would sit outside with his pint of beer, talking to the men, like an advert for the beer. I used to see him sitting out there when I went past. I suppose he was pretty old. His suit was old and bleached, as if it had been left in the sun.

All those people, the richer people, they never changed their clothes unless they went to parties. They all used to wear faded clothes! I expect they were very good quality. Say it was a green suit, it would go sort of white! They never had new suits of clothes on.

Omar Davis was a farmer at Nesley, another place on our country round but one only Gilbert delivered bread to. I never went there, and Gilbert told me about him. They wouldn't have the labourers' children in the house 'in case they heard anything'. The labourers there, and their families, didn't do very well, but all right, until one of the farmer's men asked Omar Davis for a rise.

'A rise? a rise? You can go and stand on the manure heap. That'll give you a rise!'

The Belgian gentleman who had Arthur Spurling the jockey working for him and Gilbert Pegler's relation Smith as a chauffeur lived in a big house at Nesley. He counted as a farmer, but he didn't do any farming; he had a farm; I suppose he was a gentleman farmer. Smith didn't stay there: he drove home to Tetbury every night and back again in the morning.

Shepherd Hudd (Shep Hudd) lived with his wife and his son in the middle of a field at Ozleworth (he used to call it Uzzelworth), in a cottage.

You opened a farm gate and went through a field and down to another one, and that's where the Hudds lived, in a cottage in the middle of a field.

When I brought the bread across the field to Shep Hudd and got to his house I would shout 'Baker!' He always did the same thing if he was in his cottage. I would go in and he would have what he wanted out of the basket; he would take the bread off of me - the bread was top and bottom, what they call a cottage loaf - and when he took it from me he always snatched the top off the loaf, and shoved the rest along the table.

He would get his penknife out and cut himself a little piece of cheese, only as big through as his thumb; and when he had torn the top off he held the top of the loaf and the cheese together with his finger and thumb; he would cut a piece of bread and a piece of cheese against his thumb and eat it; then he would cut another bit and give it to the cat. Then he cut several pieces for himself, and one or two for the cat, while I was there.

It's the only cat I ever saw eat bread. Or cheese, either. Shep would be sitting there in his wooden chair that was all tied up with string (that was because he was such a big fella), cutting away, eating and feeding the cat.

The cat would eat his allowance in the field, and I always thought, That's strange - because in the field there's mice about.

Mrs Hudd said that lambs and sheep and hurdles was all she ever heard of. They would use hurdles to cut off a piece of field with turnips and the sheep were allotted that to eat; and then they would build them another place. The sheep came to the market dressed with lumps of field on the ends of their tails. I expect they had been eating turnips in the fields. The shepherds didn't drive the sheep: they had to walk at the speed of the sheep.

The son, a cowman, got up and made a pot of tea at 4 o'clock in the morning. They kept that same tea going by the fire and topped it up with fresh boiling water all day long. Once Gilbert Pegler's son Malcolm came with me.

'Oos that?' Shep said to me.

'Why, it's Mr Pegler's son.'

'Allo, young Pagler!'

Shep Hudd offered him a cup of tea. He said 'Thank you,' and Shep gave him some out of the teapot. I watched as Malcolm worked his way back to the door, and when he thought the shepherd wasn't looking he pushed it out into the field. Next time I went, without Malcolm, Shep said 'I an't gi'in' he another cup of tea after what he did. My son made that at four o'clock this morning and he whizzed it out the door!' (except that what he said was much more rude than that, and there was more to it: Shep was very upset).

I would say that in all the years I was taking bread to him, Shep Hudd never once offered me a cup of tea; but, you see, Malcolm was 'young maister' to him.

As I told you he lived with his son: well, one day the father told me his son was having a *revorce*.

I took my mother the same journey once. She said 'Everyone you meet you put your hand up to!' Well, I did because I knew them all - they all got bread from me.

She saw a man hoeing in a field. It was Shep Hudd's son. She came again with me a few weeks later. The man looked as if he hadn't moved. He was in the same field doing the same thing. 'Has he been there doing the same thing all this time?' she said.

Shep Hudd knew Aunt Annie over at Bagpath. Well, every time I saw him, as soon as he had got going on his bread and cheese he would ask after her: 'How's the old crettur?' And I had to give him any news of her. People always walked, and you and I might think that it was a long walk from Bagpath to Ozleworth, and they might never meet each other, but they used to know each other once and he knew I was her nephew. People would be bound to have friends and they always talked. They walked, and they met one another and they talked. They wouldn't think it was far to walk from Ozleworth to Bagpath.

A man came to live at Ozleworth with his wife, and then he changed houses with someone at the other side of the globe - the other side of Ozleworth, anyway - and each man went to live in the other man's house with the other man's wife. The wives stayed where they were. Peglers delivered on Tuesday and Friday: my day was Tuesday and Gilbert's was Friday. One of the women had a baby on the Tuesday and I told Gilbert, and when he went on Friday he said to the man who wasn't her husband, 'I hear missus has had a baby. How is she?'

'Oh,' said the fellow, 'she's back working at the tub today.'

This is about a farm near Bagpath, when I was doing my journey in the country. It wasn't really Bagpath, it was Tilputs End. When they made a store for potatoes in those days they usually dug a pit and put the potatoes in it and covered them up. This farmer, instead of making a pit, he built walls of straw bales all round and another lot on top, and the potatoes went straight on the ground. This was quite a good way of storing potatoes and when they opened the store they were all right. But this is what happened: they covered the potatoes with whole bales of straw and then put soil over it, and the weight pushed some of the potatoes under the straw walls. When the time came to take the potatoes out, the straw bales of the walls weren't moved. Well, along came the baker, a young man called Frank, and he worked methodically along and got a whole lot of potatoes - another crop, because they were all growing!

It was a big farm, and they had a high steel fence, high up; and they bred pheasants behind the fence. They used to hang meat up on the fence and the pheasants ate the meat off the bones.

There was a girl who worked there, who married the son of the house: I used to fancy her! That's all - just fancied her. She always wore a bonnet with long flaps. All the women wore them in those days when they were working in the fields because they didn't want their face to be brown!

Once my sister Vera worked near Uley for one of her jobs as a housemaid, on the main road opposite to The Firs at Symonds Hall - Zimmerzalvirs - and I used to deliver bread there. Now I'll tell you what I found in the hedge there: some yellow cherries. I got out of the van and picked plenty. I took them home and Mother made some jam from them. It was beautiful.

Then there was another fellow I didn't know, because Gilbert always served him: when the bread arrived he was always getting half a bucket of potatoes for his dinner. He had a gift for eating! But that's all he had - potatoes.

Another fellow - I can't remember his name now - was complaining about his bad ear: 'It's my wicker!'

"Pardon?'

'Me sowse!'

Another thing he always complained about was his watch: 'There's my watch! It's no good! My clock's all right!' But the thing was, he always went by his watch, not the clock.

And another thing: he was always boasting about his cabbages: 'I keep the water that I do myself, my human water, and put it on the cabbages.'

I thought, You're flippin daft! This is all quite true.

I was delivering out there so long I saw the children grow up. There was one boy, not very bright, and he grew up and left school and went to be a labourer on the farm. He always wore a school cap to work.

And there's still things beyond all that. Sometimes it was downright dangerous when you left the van and took your basket of bread. I was chased by bullocks once and I had to get away through the hedge. They may not have hurt me but I wasn't taking chances.

Geese can be dangerous too when you're delivering to houses in the country. I was delivering to the Vicar of Beverstone once. The reverend gentleman was a well-known swearing man, and he had loads of geese. He used to swear at me and I expect he used to swear at everybody. He was always swearing. When I was trying to deliver the bread there they all came hissing round me. I didn't know what to do.

I was going back to the van when some geese ran at me, making a noise, hissing. I kept the basket in front of me because they frightened me, and got my back up to the van door and opened it without turning round. I was knocking them with my basket when they came for me. Along came the vicar, swearing as usual and telling me to 'Get away, there!' I got in still holding the basket between me and the geese.

When I drove away I ran straight over one of the geese and I thought I'd killed it as it lay flat on the road. But in the mirror I saw it get up and walk away.

A family came to Beverstone from Scotland, to a farm. They brought all their cattle and implements on the train to Tetbury and walked everything through the town and all the way to Beverstone. They had a new parlour built at the farm. I don't know if it's still in use.

When you were a baker in the country, going round the farms and cottages, you got to know other people's business. We knew everything. The baker had a different role to today.

I would leave the van with my basket and go up to the front door: Knock! knock! 'Baker!' and go straight in and they would be talking and I would talk with them, or there would be two women talking and they would pay me no more attention than anything, and I observed! I have a great head full of what I heard. You wouldn't believe what I knew, but there was nothing else to entertain us. I used to go to the house and they didn't stop talking when the baker came.

There's tons of things, every day. I knew that someone had had a baby and got rid of it because the father (they weren't married) was a foreigner.

A job I did for the people in the country was to take their glass accumulators, the wet cell batteries for the wireless, back to Tetbury to get them charged. They went in the van with the bread.

One place I delivered was a gentleman's house where you went in through the dairy. They used to kill animals there for food and they would be preparing meat in the dairy. When I had done my delivery at the house I went back to the van through the dairy and the man would say 'Here, baker!' and he would throw something into my basket that I was carrying on my back. It was always some offal. That was good.

I knew too many people's business - but you could tell anything in Tetbury, as long as they didn't know about it!

Quite often in the morning at the right time of year I would pop into a field on the way to work and look for some mushrooms. The best places were where animals had been kept, and I have been in some places early in the morning where you couldn't walk for treading on them, they were so thick on the ground. One morning I went into a wheatfield because I could see the mushrooms there, and if I moved a foot I would be on a mushroom. As I was picking them the man came up: 'What are you doing in my field?'

'Picking myself a few mushrooms.'

Well, get out straight away, because you are crushing my wheat.'

Well, I thought to myself, You must be crackers! because I knew that in a day or two he would be sending the roller in, because that's what they always did with young wheat (and in fact this man did it two days later) so what harm my feet could do I don't know. Well, I came out of his field while he stood there, but I was carrying my mushrooms!

On mornings like that we would have mushrooms with our breakfast at the bakehouse. We would have some bacon and put that with all the mushrooms in a metal tray and put it in the ordinary proper baking oven and it would soon be done and we would have a marvellous breakfast with some bread. It was smashing. In those days I would have two big pint mugs of tea with my breakfast. Then if I was going on my journey I probably wouldn't have another drink until I got home.

As I said, I sometimes took my mother with me on my journey in the country, and later, when I was married and living at Bath Road, I would take one of the boys occasionally. Now, one day I had to take out some extra bread after I had finished my journey, so when I had loaded up I took the van home first. David was back from school, and I said 'Do you want to come out with me?' Of course he did! It was only a short distance, but somehow Gilbert got to hear of it and forbade me to take any of my family with me again.

On our job we had to keep our eyes open for new people. There was a laundry at Northfield and there was a new man who had come to take charge of it, and I found where he lived and went round to ask him for his custom. When I got there and knocked on the door a dog rushed out, yapping, and I said 'Now, Pip!' - and he stopped barking.

The man said 'What did you say to the dog? What did you call it?' He thought I was grumbling, you see.

'I called it Pip,' I said. It was a terrier, a quick dog.

'Well,' the man said, 'that's his name!' He went on to say 'That's really strange. Do you know, we bought him from this town, and he was called Pip already, and we called it Pip!' He explained that he came to Tetbury from Swindon, but some time before he got the job at the laundry they had seen an advert for a fox-terrier in Tetbury and come over and bought it. Of course, this was the dog we had sold and thought we never would see again. We used to breed dogs, and this one was the last of the litter. We kept it too long and I called it Pip. It was an alert pup, very sharp, and I suppose that's why we called the puppy Pip. Anyrate, I was sure it looked like it.

I got the custom.

The beginning of winter in 1947 was in January and of course we had to go to work as usual and take bread round in the country. There was a photographer in Cirencester and he had some marvellous photos of the snow. They must still have them somewhere. They took photos of us when we were delivering bread in the street. I say we were in the street - it was the main road to Kingscote and beyond, and up on the heights, and the road was full with snow up the sides; they had cut the road out and it was as high as a rick, like a house without a lid. The roadmen had cut benches out in a hollow in the snow at the sides, and put a bale of straw in and sat on it, and they had a brazier for making their tea.

Everything was frozen. You could run about on top of the snow, even as deep as that, it was so frozen. All the gates were frozen, and we couldn't get beyond the main road. You had to bundle up some loaves in a flour sack and put it over your back and go across the field on foot because a lot of people round there lived in a house all by itself in a field, or across two fields. The people who lived there used to shovel their way to the main road, and the people who lived in a village had to do the same, only they met the roadmen on the way, and they bought them half a pint - we never got a penny piece for getting the bread through!

Another thing was that we were kind hearts, and when we found a car or a van stuck in a snow drift we would try to help them to get out, and we got some people out of the snow. But it's difficult there - the road goes up and down and they tended to get stuck at the bottom and they would get going from the bottom of the hill and then rush at it and come sliding back down. But we towed some of them and got them out. It was a dreadful sight.

The rabbits - there were lots of wild rabbits then - survived by gnawing young trees, as high as they could reach, higher than anyone would think, and robbed the bark. There were wood pigeons (what my father called quisties) high up in the trees, and the frost caught them and they were frozen to death up in the trees. They fell to the ground when it thawed. That was amazing, wasn't it? It snowed and froze from January that year to April, and on Gilbert Pegler's birthday, which was in May, there was still snow left frozen under the hedgerows. People ought to know about such things.

When the thaw came all the snow melted - the day after I had been to Bagpath - and the wet from the snow came into the rivers. In Tetbury it all flowed into the Arnold and the water went from one wall to the other, and it flowed into Wiltshire and there were floods there. I had to go through a ford near Crudwell on one of my journeys into Wiltshire. When I came to it I had nothing at the bottom of my van and the water was so deep it came right round my feet.

We always had flour for the bakehouse during that winter. We were lucky that it only had to come from Dursley, and that's nothing really; and when they were late delivering it we had quite a lot in stock to use, and we never ran out of bread to deliver to the people in the snow.

There are heaps and heaps of things I can remember about those journeys.

Now the old man, Jim Pegler, has gone. He was getting on when I started there.

He's been dead for years and years. He was always good for his age.

There's none of them there now. They've lost the job altogether. There isn't even a bakehouse there.

And Gilbert's gone, and his wife, Lizzie. She was a nice person. They lived at the shop for a while.

There were two daughters, Gladys and Nora, and the boy, Malcolm. I used to have both those two girls in the basket. I was able to carry those two very easily. I must have been strong! It wasn't the ordinary basket we used to keep in the van for taking bread into the houses. It was one you used for several deliveries where there wasn't a road and you had to do the deliveries on foot and go across the fields.

Nora Pegler married a showman with a roundabout, but sometimes he drove a lorry. Once he had an accident with a load of tea and he was charged with having an insecure load. He was prosecuted but he got off - I don't know why, perhaps because it wasn't an insecure load - it was on the ground!

I don't know what happened to Gladys.

Malcolm is a farmer. He has a few cows and stuff. The woman that Old Pegler, the old granddad, married as his second wife was an old maid, related to the Dolphin Coal and Coke Company. When he got married he moved into her nice house on the right hand side of Cirencester Road, past the Oak. They went and lived there. That is, the house Mr Pegler went to live in was his wife's house. One thing about her, the house was always very clean and tidy. Before he died she left it to Malcolm in her will, the whole house. That's the house Malcolm lives in now.

– THE SEVENTH PART –

The Rest of Tetbury

WITCHELL'S

Witchell's was the ironmonger's and general hardware shop in Church Street, where my father used to work. There may have been some connexion between the Witchells and Warn's Brewery but that was before my time. Sidney Witchell was my dad's boss.

Witchell's ironmonger's and general hardware shop where Dad worked from 1885 to 1936, first in the shop and then as a blacksmith in the smith's shop behind. The whole front has been destroyed. Now there is a horseshoe on the door to Troopers Court.

There were workshops at the back, what they call Troopers Court now - all the Witchells were called Trooper - and it wasn't very big there. They had two forges. They didn't have much, you see, but they got through a lot of work there.

I can remember Witchell's workshop before I can remember anything else. They had a roasting place to get iron tyres hot and put them on the wooden wheels of carts and waggons. I remember Dad had his left elbow on his bellows, and he was stirring the fire with a long iron until it got hot, and the other fellow, the striker, had a big hammer. My father showed him with a small hammer where to hit: da da dah! and the striker hit the iron there.

It was always a blacksmith's shop but never a shoeing smith's shop. It's disgusting, on the door of the new building where the workshop used to be there's a horseshoe on the door. There shouldn't be a horseshoe there. Nobody ever shoed horses there.

They did have a horse, to take ironwork out into the fields, but they had nothing to do with shoeing it. Dad used to go out with the cart with the ironwork, and sometimes he gave lifts to people, because that's what you did. One day he gave a lift to a man and got into conversation with him. When he got down the man said to him 'I'll give you some fruit.' Dad thanked him, and didn't think any more about it, and then a long box arrived, like an ammunition box, packed with fruit. Dad hadn't thought he meant it, and he didn't even know who the chap was. It was wonderful! It was like having a blue moon!

Once Dad had an accident with the cart, that caused him a lot of bother, and perhaps he never got over it. Someone let something go and the lot, the whole load, fell on him.

Mainly my dad used to make things for the customers. When he started there he was in the shop for so many years, as an ironmonger (that's what he was apprenticed as) and then the next few years he learned the blacksmith's trade in the workshop. He was nearly fourteen when he started there, and it was the only job he had till he retired. But he was never a shoeing smith and nor was anyone else there. You can see the photograph of Sidney Witchell as a little boy on his father's knee, with Dad as an apprentice standing at the back.

Mr Witchell junior had this picture taken soon after Dad was apprenticed to him. Dad is the second from the right at the back. The little boy at the front is Sidney, Mr Witchells son. When Dad retired Sidney was the boss, and had been for a long time.

Did you know that the cockerel on St Saviour's church was made by Witchell's?

When my father was the blacksmith at Witchell's he used to measure, not by the way they do now, but by figures - that is, not by inches: If they wanted to measure, say, across the top of a barrel, they wouldn't measure it in inches, but by a number; and the same with things they sold in the shop - they never had a price on them, but just letters. Dad knew what the price was from the letters. I think it was so that other people wouldn't see what Witchell's were charging. He worked in the shop before he did any work in the workshop, and he could always sell you things in the shop, because he was a trained ironmonger.

People used to come into the shop and ask him to make things, things that you might just go and buy in a shop now - he had to make metal barrels, for an instance, and the way he worked out the metal was, he measured the round bit at the end, and he got a piece of iron three times that in length, and that made the sides. That's what he told me.

I have been told that this picture is of Dad at work. It may be; or it may be his brother Walter when he was working for Witchell.

There were two forges in the workshop, and an anvil. I spent all my life in there with him at one time when I was little. There is a picture of him working at the forge, and you can see a horseshoe on the wall behind him. Perhaps Dad put it there for luck - I still have a horseshoe outside my back door - or it might be for forty things. The point was, no horse was ever shoed there.

Witchell's was a blacksmiths and ironmongers all my time, and my dad's time, but everyone knows it was a very old inn before it was a blacksmith's, called The Three Cups. There is a story that Sidney Witchell's grandfather committed suicide by hanging himself from the top of the newel post in his house; I don't think that's true, but I know his father shot himself in the head, with his shotgun, in the little office that used to be at the front of the shop. I know that, because Dad had to brush his blood and brains off the ceiling. In my time the business was run by Sidney Witchell and his sister, Barbara.

Sidney Witchell was a very nice man. He was very nice to us children. When the circus came to Tetbury he always gave Dad threepence for each of us in the family, so that we could 'go and see the clowns'. When the place was demolished they had the excuse that the building was ruinous, but apparently they had a hard time smashing it down. They say that the Witchells never did anything to the house and it was falling to pieces. Sidney and his sister always lived there, but if there was a thunderstorm at night they would get up and go for a walk in case everything fell down.

They were both what you would call eccentric. He would come out after he had had his dinner and go down to the workshop with his false teeth in his hand, licking them clean. They must have fit like a barge! Eddie's wife, Pat, used to work for him at one time, in the shop, and she said that if he sent a bill out it was always on a scrap of paper, not a bill-head.

The shop had all sorts of old rusty things heaped up in it, as well as the normal stock of an ironmonger. If he hadn't got anything you wanted he would find you something somewhere among the rubbish. He found me a carving knife once, but it was a great big plain steel one; all the blade was mottled, and I didn't buy it. Another time I wanted an oil-can, and he hadn't got one; but he rummaged around and came up with a second-hand Bovril jar he had saved, with a little tin spout soldered to the lid. He kept all these things in case they came in useful and he could sell them and make a profit. It was a customary thing for him to go through the rubbish to see if he could *oblige* anybody.

Edith went in one day to buy a peg bag, and he said to Miss Mann, who was his assistant in the shop then: 'A peg bag? A peg bag? Do you know what a peg bag is, Miss Mann?' But he had a great respect for Edith. She went in and asked him for matches during the war when there was a shortage and he fetched her some up from under the counter. He wouldn't have done that for most people.

You know he used to collect cabbage stumps from the field on the Long Newnton Road (before he died he owned quite a lot of Tetbury, I think - several houses at least, and several fields: that was what he spent his money on) and he would stack them criss cross in the cellar until they were dried out and he could use them for firewood.

He and his sister were well known for being mean with money. I used to deliver their bread from Peglers, and once a week they used to have a cake. One day she said to Mrs Pegler 'I won't have any more cake. I want to cancel the order.' This was during the war. Originally Peglers used to make very good cake, but in the war what Gilbert made really was horrible stuff, nothing in it, but it was all you could get if you ordered from them. And apart from Stanley Marks', that came from Bristol, all the cake in Tetbury was made by Gilbert Pegler. When I heard that Miss Witchell had cancelled it I first thought, He's had enough of it! Because it was real awful. But in fact she went on to say 'It's my brother! He's too greedy! He wants two pieces!'

I caught Sidney Witchell in the street outside the Town Hall when he was very old. He had an umbrella with not all the spars, and a basket over his arm. There's a photo that Cliff took that shows me talking to Sidney Witchell there.

SOME MORE TETBURY PEOPLE

When the war started in 1914 all the young men went and joined the army. Now, this is very conspicuous - they were all together, and they all wore caps.

Hubert Horton, Gilbert Horton's son, when he lived at the Knap, used to go out with Jack Phillips the baker and deliver bread all round late at night - creeping about at night with bread. I should think it was night and day with them. When they got to the Greyhound in Hampton Street Jack Phillips put Hubert in the 'hole', the entrance to the Jug and Bottle, and stood him a drink while he stayed in the bar drinking. Hubert, who was only a boy then, used to wait in there and wait, and when Jack came out at last they carried on delivering the bread.

The horse used to bring Jack back home, riding on the shaft of the cart, drunk. He was so drunk one night on the Rodmarton road he dropped off the shaft and the cart went over him, and that was the end of him. The horse went home without him, and they went to look for him. He was the son of the J Phillips of E & J Phillips. The other Phillips had daughters. John Phillips took over the bakehouse.

I used to ride in Hubert Horton's father's goat cart, up and down the road. It was champion. That was as kids: Hubert was a baker and I was a baker. It was a tiny cart, enough for two to sit in. It had two wheels. That would be when I was about fifteen. But sometimes before then, when we were still at school, we would go out at the end of the afternoon, and Hubert would put the harness on the goat, and get it into the shafts, and off we would go down the road, as far as Charlton.

Jim Ind used to live in the Pike House at Seven Furlong. The Warren is on the left, and Walkers used to share it with them and other families because it was common land.

Billy Purnell was the landlord's son at the Plough. Billy had the best suit in the world, but he still looked like a scarecrow. Nothing could be done to make him pretty, either.

I was at school with a boy called Tommy Hall. Some time ago I was in Tetbury and I was talking to somebody, I don't remember who, and they said, 'Here comes someone you know.'

'Nobody I know!' I said.

'You do know. I'm positive.'

'No idea who it is,' I said.

'It's Tommy Hall.'

'So it is!' And it was Tommy Hall. He was a great big ugly fellow! Tommy and his father made hurdles to keep sheep in. His father was the father of Tommy's sister's child.

There was Cocker Rich. Edith called him the Galloping Major. He used to go out on horseback with the Home Guard during the war. He was an old man, even when I knew him. He used to buy and sell horses. He used to make them do tricks on the Green. He was a handy fellow and he could do what he liked with a horse. Cocker Rich's horse would kneel down and then stand up on two legs.

He had a sister we called Miss Rich. She was what I call beautiful and she married Mr Wheeler at the White Hart Hotel. He wasn't a very nice man. I used to deliver the papers there and I was always glad to get out. The place always stunk of smoke and stale beer. How she stood the smell of the place I don't know.

Cocker Rich's other sister had a son who became an electrician. He got electrocuted up a pole. It didn't kill him, I think. It was when they were putting in electricity down Charlton Road, power wires up a post, for the

Electricity Company. He just got caught up there. Of course, electricity had only just come into Tetbury.

There were plenty of Saunderses, 'late of this parish', as you know. Their memorial is in the big church.

The Estcourt family were always in Tetbury. Raymond found a piece of a house roof and because he wondered where it was made he went and spoke to Miss Estcourt. She said 'Come in,' and she did all she could to entertain him. The thing, whatever it was, had been made there at Estcourt House where there used to be a kiln. I think it was a ridge tile, but I'm not sure. Something like that.

Isabel Parsons who worked for the Wheelers at the shoe shop was a friend of Laura's; her father worked at Warn's Brewery. That was reckoned to be a good job because Warns did extra things like bottled beer.

Something else about Warns: when Raymond had spots on his face he had to go to Warns to get some yeast, to eat it. He did eat it, and it made him better.

There were three milkmen; one was Hoppy Haine who had a cork leg, and he used to come from Long Acre; he had two dippers, a pint and half a pint, and he would shout 'Milk!' and measure it out into your can, with a little bit at the end. Reg Cleaver was a milkman once too, as well as being a blacksmith and a secretary: he went around carrying milk in a big can with measures inside and with little cans hanging from it outside. When he had to measure the milk out he put his bucket down on the ground first. And there was Simeon Long. He carried milk in a bucket.

In those days there were always food and drink inspectors around. Simeon Long always said 'Have you seen Burton?' Mr Burton used to come from Bristol to make spot checks. If there was any doubt Simeon knocked his bucket over, and then he hadn't any milk to be inspected. He probably had water in it. People had to mind their ps and qs when the inspectors were around. Simeon Long lived at Cutwell Villa with his two daughters. Livvy Long married Sam West, but they separated.

I had my bread weighed by an inspector outside Lewises once, and it was at fault. Now Mr Prescott the chemist in Church Street was what we called a big man who had a big say in things; he may have been a magistrate or something, but I don't know. Mr Pegler had to go to him when he had been reported because his loaves were short weight, but Mr Prescott said he understood. Mr Pegler had to admit it was a fault, but said he wasn't trying anything on, it was a mistake - the bread had been in the oven a long time. As far as I know, that was the end of it. This is what had happened: everyone else had gone and left me alone in the bakehouse, and I was supposed to be getting the bread out of the oven. It took a long time to get colour on. Mrs Pegler knew what had happened, too, and she knew that it took a long time to bake, and that is what Mr Pegler told Mr Prescott. I didn't get into trouble.

Persis Lamb took this picture for the Council, too. You can see Worthy Kidd's house on the right, before it had windows. To the left of number 6, down Blackhorse Hill and past the little cemetery, is West's house; further on, across the stream, is Ball's house, called Under Bath Bridge. Next door to number 6, on the right, is the barn where Mr Walker kept his circular saw. After the war it was converted into a house. At the top of the hill, on the left, is Warn's Brewery chimney.

'Roundun! Bubba! Worthy Kidd!' the children used to shout after him. His name was Worthy Kidd, and he was a very old man when I knew him. He was a bit odd, too. He was too old to be working and the children used to shout after him. Another shout you heard was 'Worthy Kidd! Worthy Kidd! Who stole the boiler lid?' I don't know why they said it. Children always seemed to shout after people in the street then. People were very rude in those days.

Mr Kidd lived with his wife in the house we lived in afterwards, during the war, 6 Bath Road, at the top of Black Horse Hill, where they used to put all the stone for mending the road. It can hardly have been a house, then. I think the house was a rubbish dump. There were only four windows, all looking towards the town, pointed windows like a church, and only a fireplace inside. It may once have had something to do with the churchyard at the bottom of the garden, but I don't know. I think Pegler bought the house when the Kidds moved to the little house across the road, behind the Brethren's church at the bottom of Bath Bridge. After Worthy Kidd died his widow lived there with a dog called Laddie. Mrs Kidd used to take a lot of snuff and her nose was always dirty and bunged up.

After Worthy Kidd died, his house, number 6 Bath Road, was condemned by the Council, but Jim Pegler had windows put in and a cold water tap as well as electric light, drains and a toilet down the garden, and he rented it to us. There were a lot of mice. The house is called The Old Toll House now. On the right you can see the stile, made of hard stile stone, that leads to the footpath through Grange Fields. We used to walk to Estcourt House and Long Newnton that way.

Mr Pegler had more windows put in: one in the living room, one in the bedroom, one very small one on the landing and another in the pantry; and a cold tap; and an oven in the chimney breast.

They put a water closet down the yard, too, and connected us up to the sewers, but not very well. There was a bad drain in the yard. Another Mr Smith, who was the husband of Mrs Daily Mail Smith, had to unearth it when it flooded. I think the surveyor, Mr Hearling, did something wrong. He let someone cover the drain up, and he didn't do it properly. The man had to come back because there was a burst and a flood that damaged some of our stuff that was in the shed when we were moving in, including some photograph albums. Before Pegler bought it, the house was condemned!

A few years ago I went to see Mrs Jones, Ada Jones, at The Priory. She used to live opposite us in Bath Road with her husband and the family. They sold us a boy's bicycle for John when he was seven. Mr Jones, Bert, used to drive a horse for Phillips. They used to get corn from a mill company in Hull called Paull's and he would deliver it to people who had chickens and so on. He used to come home for his dinner and tie the horse up to the fence by our house with a nosebag on.

Anyrate, while I was in there, in The Priory, there was a lady there and she said to me 'Excuse me, do they call you Frank Peters?' When I said yes, I was, she said 'I remember you as a bright young lad. You were a lovely little boy. You used to work for Pegler, and you brought the bread in a basket. I saw you with your white hair, going round Tetbury delivering bread, going up and down.' Well, she didn't say who she was, and I didn't ask her, but afterwards I realised who she was. She was Worthy Kidd's granddaughter who used to live with them at Bath Road. She married the horrible policeman. My sister Rene would have known her. 'I'm ninety years old!' she said to me. I can't understand how she knew me. I didn't know she was interested! She must have been older than me. I think one of us must have been early and the other late, or one before and the other behind!

Bill Wiltshire was a cowman for Keevils at Upton. He lived with his mother and father and you could hear her shouting: 'Come on, Bill! Gert on!' She was in a bathchair, a basket chair, and her husband (his name was Bill, too) would tow her ('Faster!') on his bicycle, all over the place. 'Come on, Bill!' she would shout, 'can't you go faster?' They were both odd - they must have been!

Dennis Price lived down in Cutwell, on the bank above the stream - one of those houses. He trained the horses for the War. They had a lot of horses in the first World War, you know, and he had to run with them. The horses he passed, they had in the War.

Mr Pockett had a garage. He was a good friend to me. He was a mechanic and an inventor. He used to live up Love Lane. There were two cottages: Chummer Smith, who came to Hull later, working in a factory, lived in one, and Barnes in the next, and then there was Pockett's. He built his house himself with mortar he dug out of the side of the road at Petty France.

You know, he invented dipping headlights. A man who had a heavy car came to him in tears because he had got into a row. A farmer had threatened him - said his car lights frightened the cows at night - and Mr Pockett modified his car so that when he moved a lever like a brake lever the headlights swivelled down and changed position. He didn't patent it. I don't suppose he even knew about things like that in those days. The story is that the man who had the car took it into a garage - I think it was Steel's Garage in Cirencester - and the mechanic came to start the car and came to take the handbrake off to move the car, and it wouldn't move. The handle he had moved wasn't the handbrake: it was a handle that controlled the headlights, made them go up and down, dipping them. They inspected the car to find out what was wrong, gave it a real thorough inspection, and realised how it had been changed. Of course, it wasn't electric, it was mechanical. Then someone patented dipping headlights, and it wasn't Mr Pockett.

He had a device on his car to open his gates, too. When he got to the top of Love Lane he did something in his car and the gate opened where he lived. He was very clever. He made a lot of clever things. Some of the things he made are in the museum at Gloucester.

He used to deal with Morgan three-wheelers - he sold one to Gilbert Pegler. He was a kind man and a clever man, but he was a silly man, too. You know, he even built himself a Morgan. He had one but he built a lot of it himself. You know the engine on a Morgan was on the front of the car, and as he was driving along he used to watch the engine. If anything went wrong, or he heard anything, he always tried to adjust it as he was going along. He wouldn't stop. One day he was driving along, watching the engine; he had Reg Cleaver with him that day and he was so busy doing it that he went up the bank and into the hedge. The car went over, though neither of them was hurt.

He was a faithful man. He used to smoke every morning when he was getting dressed, and every night when he got undressed. He was converted and joined the Exclusive Brethren. When he found he was the only one in the Meeting that smoked he said 'I'll give it up, then!' and he did.

When I first knew him he was married to a woman who was not a bad woman. She would help anybody. One day Mr Pockett was working on a car down the yard from his house, at the end of his long garage, banging away, and he heard Gilbert Pegler chatting to his mates in the road. Now, Mr Pockett was a man who always seemed to be able to hear and work at the same time, and what he heard was Gilbert Pegler running Mrs Pockett down! Mr Pockett came down and spoke to him and that was that.

Later on, his wife died; he got with another woman, one of his customers, who was a cook at one of the houses. It was all respectable, but the Brethren found out, and when they knew she wasn't a Brethren he was put out - because of the woman!

Ellis Pockett, who was known as Jimmy, was Mr Pockett's son. He wasn't very well, but he was my friend. They called him 'Simple Pockett', like Simple Simon, but he was clever in his way, like his dad's way. Jimmy let me have a ride on his motorbike that was out of the ark - it was the first motorbike I ever rode. He was good with his hands, and he made a crystal set wireless, what they called a cats-whisker, but he couldn't get much on it. Now, the houses they lived in were a row, and in the roof there wasn't a division between the houses - no wall between them and next door. The houses were all in one under the roof. So he went up there with a wire for the aerial and he put the aerial from end to end, inside, and ran it down the row! I wonder if anyone has found it yet? The other people in the row didn't know about it then. I think he was a clever lad.

Once I went to Cherington Pond to have a swim with him. We sometimes went out together, where nobody would know us. We would get hold of something to ride or drive. We went in the water, though I couldn't swim. He was an ill kid and if he saw a girl coming he would say 'Are my feet straight?' because he had crippled feet. Well, the day we went to Cherington I found some keys there. To be quite honest, when I got dressed I picked them up off the ground, where Jimmy had chucked his clothes off, but I didn't know they were his - I didn't give it a thought.

Now, Jimmy used to have to go and do something to the fire engine where it was kept in the shut up part under the Town Hall every day, to get it ready to start. It wasn't a motor fire engine, it was a horse-drawn one. At that time his father was a fireman, and Mother's cousin Taylor, who kept the sweet shop at the corner of Silver Street and Market Place, was the main fireman. Jack Warn the brewer was in charge of the horses. On the keys was a label and written on it something like IF YOU FIND THIS KEY TAKE IT TO TETBURY. FINDER WILL HAVE A REWARD OF FIVE SHILLINGS.

Jimmy said, 'You take them back yourself. You found them! There's a reward for anyone who hands it in - you might as well have it!' and I did and got the five shillings. There was somebody's address on the label, the address of one of the firemen - one of the bosses. I don't remember now who it was, but I took it back and handed it in the next day and got the five shillings. I got a message from one of the firemen, too. The key opened the engine house under the Town Hall. And usually Jimmy had the key in his pocket!

His father was a very decent bloke to me. I'll tell you this story: this happened in Cheltenham, when I had my Rover. I was going down a street and a car came towards me from the right into the main street. He should have put the brake on. He was coming up to me, so I decided to turn left out of his way; but he came straight out across the street. He was so vitally near to me, but he came on, across, and ran into the side of the Rover. Dad mended my car, but a few days later I got a letter that was supposed to come from the police. The supposed policeman wrote that 'if I paid they would put it right with me'. I think it was a friend of the fellow who ran into me. I took the letter and showed it to Mr Pockett. He said, 'Leave it to me and I'll see it's put right.' I never heard anything more about it. Mind, if it was true they would have written again, wouldn't they?

When I first brought Edith to Tetbury I took her to see Mr Pockett and he said to me 'You ought to take your young woman out in the car and show her places.'

'Well,' I said, 'I haven't got a car now.'

'You can borrow this one!' he said. It was an Austin Seven, and I took her to Oxford in it. That was a whole day's journey, there and back, in those days. We had a picnic on the way.

We were having a picnic when Edith took this picture of me in the Austin Seven that Mr Pockett lent us for our day out to Oxford.

The Pocketts lived in Northfield, and further on was the shop (it sold everything) that was run by a man, Mr Sparrow, and his daughter. They had another job altogether, as well: they played music - he played the trumpet and she played the piano - for the films that showed that little fellow with the hat and the walking stick - Charlie Chaplin. It was very funny. That was when they showed the films in the upstairs room of the White Hart, the room that looked at the Town Hall, before there was a cinema in Tetbury.

Eric Vick and his sister were butchers and they kept their slaughterhouse up at Northfield, too, before ever they had the shop in London Road. They didn't have a shop of their own; they sold meat to people from the place they had. Sometimes I went to help them kill the pigs - people didn't like helping to kill pigs, I don't know why - and make sausages.

Reg Cleaver lived in West Street and he went to the Brethren's Meeting, too. He was supposed to be my friend. Reg was a blacksmith most of his life but when he was young he was a milkman. Reg used to be Mr

Pockett's secretary in his spare time. But he was usually a blacksmith. He started work with my Dad, working at Witchells. He was Dad's striker. Once, when he was working with Dad he was melting some stuff - I think it was lead - and he tried spitting in it and he burned his face. Fancy spitting in it! When he left Witchells he went to Nailsworth and took the Council job and did all the blacksmithing there.

Reg learned the trade of blacksmithing with my father, at Witchell's, but Dad was never satisfied with Reg as a workman.

After the war, after years when we had left Tetbury, we came back to see Mother, and I heard that Reg Cleaver was still working at Horsley as a Council blacksmith, and I went to look for him at the workshop where he worked. I heard he had saved every halfpenny, and he had bought two cottages; he lived in one with his wife, and their daughter and her husband lived in the other. I went down to him. He seemed embarrassed and he said (because he didn't know what to do with himself) 'W-w-what are we going to do? I can't talk to you here. I'm at work!' This was years later, as I said.

So I said 'I'll wait until five o' clock and speak to you then.' And I hung about until he came out of work and he was quite ready to talk then, and friendly. He gave me his address: St Judes, Horsley. I went up there next day and while I was looking over the car at a house to see if I had got the right place - he didn't tell me a road or a number - his daughter called out 'Hello, is that Mr Peters?' I hadn't seen them for years.

You know, Reg Cleaver wasn't really a friend. I knew that he would always 'do it' on me. I'll give you one example: one evening we were coming back from the church (that was when it was in Union Street, at the top of Gumstool Hill) and we walked down Long Street together, which we often did, and when we came to the bottom of Long Street, by Mrs Holland's house, and we were talking, he said 'I have to go now - I have something to do - I have to rush home,' and he left me. But he went back up Long Street. Now, he should have turned left, because his usual way home was up New Church Street, and he lived just round the corner of West Street, and I thought, I wonder what he's doing? Well, I raced up Eccles Court and up to the top by the Market House, and I hid behind a pillar and I saw him still strolling up Long Street. He hadn't got there yet. I stayed behind the pillar and watched. He had gone to wait for Kitty Pockett, Mr Pockett's daughter, when she came out of Harvey's Stores in Church Street. She worked there. I thought there was something on by the way he spoke to me and went back up the town. But he didn't tell me. Of course, he didn't marry Kitty - he married Rosie.

Poor old Reg! We still knocked about together, because we both had motorbikes. Neither of us had a car then, though I bought the Rover soon after, and he didn't have a car till after the war.

His father drove the brewery dray for Warn's, and if you were going to Malmesbury on the right day he would always give you a lift.

I always spoke to Ralph Cleaver, Reg's older brother. He had a motorbike, too.

Ralph was in the other Meeting, the Open Brethren at the Garret in Long Street; their parents were Baptists. Ralph worked for Topps, the bakers behind the Town Hall. He drove the van. He used to go to Bath every day in the van and fetch the cakes and confectionery from Stanley Marks (who had Topps' business afterwards) to sell in the shop. He 'dropped', we called it; that is, he used to tell a few fibs, especially about getting business. He would say, 'It's no good anyone trying to get an order there, because Topps have got it.' And it wasn't always true.

I remember when he said it about Westonbirt House, which was a gentleman's house, Sir George Holford, and then it became a school. 'We have got the bread order for Westonbirt,' he told me. But I soon knew that wasn't true. I repeated what he had said to Gilbert Pegler. Now, you would always solicit new people for their order; and the next day Gilbert came into the bakehouse and said, 'We've got Westonbirt House business now!'

The school Bursar was a man called Bunny Apperton, and I think Gilbert had come to an arrangement with him to buy all the bread they needed - and that was a lot for a boarding school - and put down for more than they had. Anyrate, the fellow that delivered the bread from Pegler's to the school (that was me) every so often took a special cake for Mr Apperton when he received the bread. Maybe he shared more than a cake. Maybe two people had a share.

Another Phillips brother lived at the bottom of Gumstool Hill, and he had a son, Albert, one of those silly fellows, a kid I used to go to school with, who went into the Home Guard in the second world war. One morning in the war, as I was going to work, it would be about four o'clock in the morning, because that's when I used to go to work at Pegler's, I had just got up to the Post Office in Church Street when Albert shouted out 'Halt! Who goes there? Friend or foe?' to me. That was him on duty in the Home Guard, guarding the Post Office. Of course I told him, 'Frank Peters' and he told me to pass. If I had said 'Foe,' he'd have shot me, wouldn't he?

And he knew who it was, because I went past every morning at that time. The point was this: Albert was absolutely timid. If anyone of any consequence had shouted at him another time he'd shit his trousers!

Fred Hills, Olive's husband, was a policeman in the war, as well as working for Holborow's, a special constable. He guarded an airfield. I don't know how he became a special. He used to run back home at night because he was nervous. There was a place where a man had been murdered, in a field between Tetbury and Long Newnton, where he lived, and he always ran past the spot if it was night time. They gave him a gun to take home, but I think that if a cow had looked at him over the hedge he would have had the same trouble as Albert! Fred was a nice man. I got on well with him.

The Tetbury Town Crier starts off: 'Hello! Hello!' and gets a crowd round him. There's always a lot of funny folks around him. Then he shouts 'A sale! a sale!' and then he goes round the town with his bell, and tells you where the sale is going to be, at such and such a time. He's out in the street when there's anything to be sold. But it's not just selling things, it's everything people should know, like the telly does now. When he had finished what he had to say he would ring his bell again: 'God Save the King!' - and always ended with 'God bless you!'

I can see his rosy face. He's all dressed up, like a soldier, in red and stuff. I remember him very well.

Bert Bignell was often with me when we were kids. He was Gale's errand boy before me, and when he left school he went to work at Robert Street's garage in Long Street. He hadn't been there long before he knew all the business! I was talking to him one day and I asked him 'Why do some cars have a plate at the back with GB on it?' I really didn't know, and it was quite rare then to see one.

'Oh,' he said, 'it means four-wheel brakes!' (that was something else rare in those days when cars usually had the footbrake operating only on the front and the handbrake on the back two wheels). But Bert knew, didn't he?

Tisty Newman was older than me. People used to call him 'the gutter-boy'. He was a poor lad, and he couldn't speak properly. He was disgusting in his habits and I don't think he ever went to school. He was a ragtime, stupid person.

There was another chap, and I can't remember his name now, who wasn't worth tuppence. Although I can't remember his name I remember his mother's name: Keziah (that was Jemima's sister in the Book of Job). He was never clean - he was a filthy fellow. I never had much to do with him; his family, who were a set of people who looked after a lot of their own, didn't care for him. The point of the story is this: many years later, when I was working at Alfred Smith's sulphur factory in Hull, he turned up, and I didn't recognise him until I heard him telling somebody 'I come from Tetbury.' I still didn't have any more to do with him than I had to.

Tom Baker was a horseman. He used to ride horses for whoever he worked for. His daughter was Mrs Smith at the chip shop in Church Street. Her husband, Harry Smith, got the money to start the shop from compensation: he lost his arm in a machine when he was working up on a stack at the farm. He got some money. The Smiths were very nice people.

Mr and Mrs Handoll used to walk up our street, Upton Road, under the trees, looking proud, him all shiny and all dressed to death in his military uniform, past our house, coming from Northfield for a walk. If you go up to Northfield, along London Road, and before you get to the end of the road where it turns right into Northfield, instead of going right you look over the wall to the left: there is the New Pond. That is where Mrs Handoll got in, to try and drown herself. It was in the evening time that she did it, because she couldn't get out by herself in the day.

She intended to do it, I don't know why, and she was successful.

Mervyn Handoll was a boy at school with me, and there was another boy, Fred, and a sister, Irene. I used to think about Irene Handoll a lot. I liked her but I never said. I went up to the door once without speaking! Mervyn had more than one child. If you go to the top of Love Lane and go down to The Oak, Gilbert Pegler lived in the last cottage and the Mervyn Handolls lived in the one next to last.

The men - never the boys - used to go round the town and sing the Gloucestershire carol: 'Wassail, wassail, all over the town, may God send our maister a good crop of carn! A-a goo-ood cra-ap of carn A-as ever you see!' I don't remember it all now, and I don't suppose they still do it. They all came from West Street. They were the drinking people, and that affected their voices. They came in the evening round the shops, when the shops were still open, to sing to the shopkeepers and the customers. They would go up and down Long Street and all over the town. I remember them when I was working at Gale's shop. They would gather in the shop doorway and sing the carol. They had an animal's head - a cow's head, I think, or something - done up and fastened on a tray. It was a custom.

Apart from that, most Tetbury carol singers were boys and very young men. We would get dressed up and have a lantern on a pole, and we always had someone who could sing! There would be several lads, and we called on houses and farms all round Tetbury. We always went to Doughton when Colonel Henry lived at Highgrove, and they would ask us into the big room and we sang there for them. Apart from me there was always Cecil Dickens, whose family came from Cirencester, and usually Guy Holland (he was one of the boys who got whipped by Charlie Brown for climbing that time Eddie escaped whipping); and some others. Several of us.

One time when we got out to Doughton we called on a fellow, Colonel Henry's son, who lived at the big farm house across the road from Highgrove, opposite. They were having a party, and they were all dressed up. Now the singers upset him because we were grinning at the way he was dressed, and he said 'Where have you come from?' and we said 'Tetbury!' and he said 'Well, go back there!'

There was one chap who was quite old who used to go round and sing carols when he wanted some money. His name was Albert Pontin, but everybody called him Albie.

He always wanted pennies, and people would give him a penny - not more - and when he had twenty four he would go to a shop for silver. He went to Peglers when Olive was working there in the shop with his two hands together, holding twenty four pennies, and she would oblige him with a two-shilling piece. He held the money in his hand (and he could hold up to twenty pennies in one hand) in case someone took it from him! He took it to the shop because, he said, he wanted it changed. Olive laughed like anything. But she would do it for him. She liked him. Everybody liked him. You know what they said about what he did with the pig when the band went by? Put it on the wall to watch! I don't know if that's true, but that's what they used to say.

Although he was quite old he still lived with his parents at the lodge at Boxwell, where Laura worked as a nursery maid. He wanted to come to Tetbury, so he would only be walking in, and if he found the butcher on the way he would ask for a lift, and if he couldn't get a lift he would make the pony trot and run along after it. Albie trotting behind a trap! Because the butcher didn't always want to give him a lift. If he wanted to go back to Boxwell he would keep an eye on the butcher, and allow him to make his calls before he asked him. And if he didn't get a lift he would make the pony trot and trot too. He could trot like a younger man.

I used to trot down Fox Hill and up Malmesbury Road to meet Mother when she went to visit our relations in Malmesbury. Albie was at the bottom of the hill when he got his lift.

He was a strange fellow: one way he was alert, and another he was daft. One day he was down at the bottom of Fox Hill and he wanted to get to Malmesbury. A man came with a cart - there were a lot of horses and carts then, and not much other traffic - and this man met him and said to him 'I have to go to the lime kiln. Do you know where it is?'

'Oh, yes,' Albie said. 'I'm going that way myself. Give me a lift and I'll tell you where it is!' The chap agreed, and Albie got up on the cart and off they went, over the bridge and past the end of the railway line, up the hill, through Long Newnton, and they went on till they came to Malmesbury. 'I get off here,' Albie said, and the chap stopped and Albie got down.

"Where do I go from here?' the chap said.

'Well,' Albie said, 'you know where you picked me up, don't you? Well, you go just over the bridge and where the railway lines come up to the road, that's the lime kiln!' He had let him take him to Malmesbury, and he was right by the lime kiln already. It was only five miles each way, but Albie got there. He was quite all right, not nasty. I remember him very well.

The Pontins were a family, just the same as everyone else. He was their son, and people treated him as that. He was crackers, but very nice.

Mr Price lived in Chavenage Lane and he had a cart. He used to go to Bristol with it and bring stuff back with him, fish mainly, and as he came along the road he shouted 'Fish! fish!' and people would come out and buy it. He knew how to shout: they called him 'Whispering Charlie Price'. It was very quiet in the country - even the sky was quiet - and when I was at Upton Road I could hear him shouting 'Fish!' when he got to Doughton. That was how quiet it was in my day.

Dr Braybrooke had the practice in Silver Street. He was a handsome man and handsome in his behaviour. I first knew him when he came out of the Air Force. His brother was the Vicar of Bagpath and got the sack from the church because he misbehaved. Dr Braybrooke became known as a clever doctor after he cut Tom Baker and opened him out and made him better. I can't remember now what was wrong with him, but the town was full of it at the time.

Edith was ill once and she saw Dr Braybrooke. Well, for a start, he came to the house to see her; that was all right, and we paid him. But he came again, when I was at home, and we said 'What has he come for?' Because you didn't want to pay again!

But he said, 'I have come as a friend - there is no question of paying. I have a friend in Bath who would like to examine you and give an opinion.'

We told him, 'We can't pay him!'

'Stop!' he said. 'What about five shillings?'

'I could afford that,' I said.

"If you can give him that he will take her.'

So he took her to a hospital in Bath, in his own car; and the other doctor saw her, and advised her what to do (it included drinking Guinness) and she did what she was told and she was well in a short time.

The last time I saw Dr Braybrooke I saw him outside the Wickham's at the Chipping when he was very old and bent right over. He always called at Wickham's house - he had married Mrs Wickham's daughter. Mrs Wickham was the widow of Dr Wickham. They used to have a dog that bit my leg once, and Doctor Wickham attended to it - he burned the bite. Someone, not me, had been annoying the dog but it bit me!

Anyrate, there he was, and I was too bashful to speak to him.

Mrs Spurling was one of my customers in Chipping Steps. I went to school with her son, Arthur Spurling. One day she came to the door with her money, to pay me. She paid every so often. Like a lot of my customers she had a book and I had to enter how much bread she had had. Today it came to four shillings, a lot of money then, and she handed me the book with the money in it. But she nearly had a fit - when I opened the book, there wasn't any money in it! She said 'But I've just put it in there!' You see, she handed the book to me closed, and I opened it, expecting that her money was in it, and it wasn't, and she had no idea where it had gone. We searched everywhere for it, both of us, and to cut a long story short, she didn't find it, but I did. It was in the turnups of my trousers, two florins, and it fell out of the book when she handed it to me.

Mr Spurling, her husband, was a jockey, a little man, who worked at Nesley.

The first big house at the top of Chipping Steps was Mr and Mrs Godwin. They were the parents of Godwin the electrician. They had retired to Tetbury from Westonbirt.

The Reverend Thompson was Vicar of Tetbury when I was a boy. He held a good part of the town by himself - he owned it, and that was about his drop. Everything was for himself, and what he wanted. He lived in the Vicarage, a very big house by the Green, in Church Lane, handy for the church. When he came out during a service to read his lessons he would give out his movements. I always noticed, if it was something he liked doing, like the Womens Institute, he would say 'I will be there,' but if it was something you would think he should be at, such as a service in the week, he would say 'I shall not be there!' But if there was money in it he would be there.

I was in the Post Office with my savings book and a pound to pay in one time, and the Parson was in there too. 'Now, Peters,' he said to me, 'what are you doing? Take it all out and put it in again! You can make fifteen shillings into a pound in the Post Office! It's compound interest!'

Reg Cox went to live in that big house past Cutwell. His father was a builder and lived further up, towards Twelveacres. Reg was a builder too. He was at school with me, in the same class. Whenever we met afterwards he always used to say, 'Hallo, Frank, ow be then? and ow do ee like your job?' When he was young he worked for my friend Charles Hedges, like I did. This is the story of a car that stopped at Nailsworth. Reg was tall then, and he didn't fit in the car very well, and as he was driving through Nailsworth one day he accidentally touched something with his knee and switched everything off, and it stopped. The car stopped. Well, he thought it had stalled and he tried to get it to go and it wouldn't. He didn't get it going. He telephoned to Tetbury for somebody from a garage to come out - it's funny, as if he had broken down in London or somewhere - and somebody came out. They saw what was wrong and switched it back on, and it just started.

I remember the man who did the hedges along the roadsides. He lived at Brokenborough. In the war the German prisoners did it.

There was a roadman too, and he worked for the Council. As he went along the road he would stop at every twitch and turn to pick up rubbish, dig weeds out of the road and so on, using his roadman's tools, of course. He lived in Tetbury but I don't remember his name.

After Charles Hedges left Tetbury he sold the builder's business to a family called Jenkins in Charlton Road who were builders. That's another family - I knew all of them, and Charlie Jenkins was at school and in the Cubs with Clarence. They were friends for a long time. He came to look for Clarence when we had a family party in Tetbury in 1994, but Clarence had died by then. I had a talk with him.

Frank West bought the cattle and the dairy in Charlton Road from Mr Hedges and he went to live at the Pike House there. He used to be a terror at school. The teacher put him over the desk to thrash him. Yet he owned Hedges' milk round afterwards. And do you know, he would sometimes put bad milk in the bottles and leave them on the step and hope you wouldn't notice.

CHILDREN AND BABIES

You would think, wouldn't you, that living in the country and having all the animals around us, especially dogs and rabbits, we would have understood about babies, but we didn't. In a way I suppose you could call us innocent, though I think they kept these things from us deliberately. I remember more than one of my brothers being born, and Laura, and each time my mother was expecting a baby they told us that she was ill and had to go to bed, and we just took that as truth. Then they told us that someone was coming with a black bag, and there would be a baby. And then it did! We didn't know the first thing!

I remember being told that my mother was ill in bed, and I had to be quiet. They said they were going to give her a bowl of gruel. And then the nurse came to the house, and she was carrying a black bag - the same one each time - and a bit later we heard a sound like a baby crying!

But then, when the baby was born, they treated it in a peculiar way. It was dressed in long clothes, hanging down, and it had its head and face all covered up, whether the mother was carrying it or it was in the pram; and a lady would say, 'Oh, Mrs Peters! your new baby! May I have a look?' and she would unwrap its little face and the lady would say 'Oh, what a pretty baby,' or whatever. I'm sure the baby could have done with some air to breathe - it can't have done any good with its face covered up, can it?

When Mother was having another baby they always got a woman in to look after us. When Clarence was being born it was a young woman - I suppose she was young, anyway, called Bessie Ball. We were horrible to her, Eddie and I. We treated her very badly and teased her so that she couldn't stand it. One day she got so angry with us that she went after us and chased us out of the house, Eddie and me, all the way from our house up the road to Upton, and then she came after us down the road saying what she was going to do with us. She chased us nearly to Avening and then we got past her and she chased us back down to Chavenage Lane and then back up the road to Tetbury, and she nearly had us when we got to the big house, Wisteria Cottage, and she was still coming after us.

Next door, before you get there coming from Avening, there was a big place for wagons. Fred Medcroft was working there and we said 'Can you lock us in the chicken shed?' and he did, and took the key away. She came in and Fred Medcroft stopped her. She knew we were in there and she wanted to know why the door was locked, and she said 'Where's the key? How did they get in?' and he pretended that he didn't know.

She was seething! She nearly turned the chicken house over, trying to get at us, but he stopped her and she didn't manage. She was promising to wallop us if she could get at us, and I'm sure she would have. But, you know, she went away, and it got squared up, and she forgot it.

I can't remember now exactly how it all ended. But we were really horrible to her.

Not all children in Tetbury were so innocent as we were; there was a man who had a shire horse, for breeding, and he took it round the farms, for the mares. Now, I don't know how they lived, but I think they must have been just anyhow and done what they wanted in the house; because he had a boy and a girl, brother and sister, and one day (it was when we were living at Bath Bridge) they were in the field, supposed to be playing with each other, and they were playing with each other, like a man with a woman. Well, I didn't like it, but I didn't know what to do about it, so I went indoors and brought Edith out and she spoke to them and they stopped and went away. But they were just ignorant of how to behave, and I think they learned what they did from their mother and father.

A COUNTRY BOY

It's a different world!

When I was a boy we would go down to Ledgemore when Fred Medcroft was working there and ask permission to pick a bunch of primroses, and we would take them back for Mother.

At one time in West Street people had birds in boxes at the top of their walls. They thought a lot of them. The sorts of birds I mean were things like chaffinches, which will live in a box, and thrushes. Thrushes make a lovely, charming song.

When we were near Chavenage House one day there was a moorhen having a race around the field, and I brought that home. When you come near to a moorhen, it dives under the water. I got it from by Cromwell's bath. It was all full of mud and water, then, but it was supposed to be a proper bath. It had a couple of steps going down to it. It was nothing to do with feeding animals. Well, I took the moorhen home and put it in a tub. But it went away.

Another time, once, I tied up a lot of finches in a nest - young ones, you know - to see what would happen. I tied them all together with string. The old bird undone all of them and unpecked the string and they all got away.

We used to go after birds' nests, all along the hedges and down by the ponds and the river, and we didn't rob the nests - we only took one egg from each nest. I knew all the different nests - they say that a blackbird is a thrush, but they don't nest in the same place, and one lines the nest and the other doesn't - and we would take all sorts of eggs and bring them home. The water-hen lays up to twenty eggs, but they often go bad - you can get a whole clutch that are all bad - and of course they are difficult to get at and you always get wet. So what we did was to get the longest stick we could and try to tip the nest up a bit so that one egg went into the water. If it floated we reckoned that most of them were probably bad and we didn't bother going for them. Clever, weren't we?

And when we brought our eggs home our sister Irene would cook them for us.

We used to walk round the fields and look for things, and inspect everybody's apples, you know, and we always took a box with us with a front that let down, in case we found something. One day we got a young family of jackdaws, and took them home with us, in the box. 'What are these doing here?' Mother said when she saw them. She would be sad for me keeping them in a box. My word! They had to go!

My mother was a kind woman, but she would kill anything. She wrung their necks, just like that, and said 'Don't bring any of these home again!' She was used to it - she was a country girl.

People often kept animals. Prices in Upton Road had a young fox once. They tried to keep it as a friend, as a pet - but when the season came it went.

Mrs Medcroft used to have a dove that lived in the house always, with the door open. It used to sit on the pictures hanging on the wall. It didn't say much, but it did a lot!

Another thing you used to see and you don't now is those insects, hard as iron - stag beetles - and they used to catch them the same way as catching bats - with your cap, throw it into the air. A stag beetle would come, say out of a pile of manure, like a fly as big as your thumb, and if it hit you on the head you would know. It might even knock you out. If you saw one that had been caught it would be crawling with its own livestock. There was another sort of insect they used to catch that you never see now - glow worms. They used to put them in their bicycle lamps (not electric ones then) and they used to glow there at night.

When I was working at Down Ampney I used to get my hair cut on a Saturday night. I would go down the road on my bike and I would get covered with midges till I was black. I have never seen so many midges since.

While we are on about insects, you ought to know that my Dad could cut flies in two with a knife. He was very cunning and very quiet and he would position his sharp knife over a fly and then bring it down quickly and that was it! We used to deal with them in the bakehouse a different way - we used to pinch their heads off when they landed on the jam tarts!

You have seen the photograph of Johnny-in-the-morning with his cart and his donkey? I know that man and I know what he used to shout as he went on his rounds. It was something like this:

'Owsellallsortsaltladies!' He came from Shipton Moyne originally, like Mother and Dad, and he slept in his cart. You know Mrs Kitcat, the solicitor's wife from London Road? You know I said I knew someone who sold her a pony? Well, it was Johnny-in-the-morning. His main job was selling salt from door to door. That was the way people used to buy salt then. There was none of the packets of 'table salt'. He had blocks of salt about fifteen or sixteen inches long and eight inches square and when he sold it he sawed off a bit with a saw. That's how you bought it.

Johnny-in-the-morning used to go round Gloucestershire and Wiltshire selling salt and donkeys and ponies. He sold a pony to Mrs Kitcat.

When I was working in Pegler's bakehouse we bought the whole block and we had a saw too. We had to cut off a lump of salt and weigh it. We had to store several blocks at a time.

Sometimes, but seldom, you would still see people taking the cow out for a walk along the road, on a rope, to get it some food. People had one cow or two. Uncle Austin had two, I think, but then he got the piece of field next to his garden to keep them in. Before that they used to walk them. They went along the grass verge, of course they did - and a lot of cars didn't knock them down! When the weather was such they would cut grass at the road side, and take it home for the cow. They never fed them at all like they do now, with artificial food, especially dead sheep. It was all grass. Some farmers would chip mangel worzels for them. Walkers had a machine for doing it.

Farmers used to take a sack of locust beans down to the field where the sheep were, and they would cuddle the sheep and give them some beans, and leave the rest in the trough for them when they went away. Then we would go and get them out of the trough and eat them ourselves. Lovely!

When they took the pigs and sheep to market, you know they didn't carry them: they had to walk there. Sheep go at less than a funeral speed, and if you had six pigs you would need six people. People don't believe you if you talk about that day, but people did it all the time like that.

Everything was good in those days. They didn't feed animals the way they do today, with all sorts of rubbish. For instance they had pigs, lovely pigs: you used to give them a bucket of barley meal and a bucket of water, throw them into the trough, and you could hear them grunting as they got into it - grunt grunt. People fed horses with corn, too. In the road there were no other tracks but where the horses had been, nothing but horse manure; and when the horse had passed all the birds flew down from the trees and picked the grain out. There were all sorts of birds, too, that you don't see now, like goldfinches - heaps of them, wherever there were horses, because of the grain.

We had some nice times, you know. Once we went on a paper chase, all around Chavenage. We were running ahead, and we went right in front of the window of the big house, Chavenage House, and we thought they would never follow us there, but they did. Eventually we got back to Tetbury, to the top of Blind Lane, and we couldn't see anyone following us. By the time we got there we thought we would be a long way ahead. So we had a rest there, and that's when they caught us.

Another thing we did when we were littluns was going swimming: the field with the pond was on one side of Upton Road and on the other side there was a wheatfield going up. Well, one day we were in the pool - it was one that filled up by itself and it probably had half a load of cow muck in it - and the farmer came along and called and shouted 'Get out of there, you boys!' and we jumped out of the water and picked up our things and ran away from him across the field with nothing on at all, as far as we could get, carrying our clothes, and run to get away from him and his stick.

You can go right to the end of Blind Lane and you come to Warner's orchard. We would go down there in the summer and call at their front door. We would put our cudgels to the side of the door and when the man came we would say 'Can we have a look in your orchard for some windfalls, please?'

He always said 'Yes, but only windfalls - don't knock any down!' and he went indoors. So we took our cudgels with us and went into the orchard. We had what we wanted, pears and apples. You would think we never had any grub!

You know, all those years ago the weather wasn't at all like it is now. I mean that in the right season it didn't rain; but often the roads that weren't tarmacked leaked water from the bottom, there was so much water round Tetbury. It was always hot in the summer.

In the winter it was different - you got a lot of rain then, and it was very cold. I remember one day in particular when it rained, and it froze all night and the house was like that, covered with ice, in the morning. And the road was covered with ice - you couldn't walk on it. When I had to go to work in the morning I had to walk in the gutter. I had to be very careful! I was very young then. I wouldn't do it now.

But it was a grand job, and we enjoyed our life. People weren't miserable but they didn't have anything.

Wood pigeons were useful. If I got one I took it home. My mother (or Edith after I was married and driving for Pegler again) would make it into a pie. But when I was young I would set up the garden riddle on its edge, and prop it up with a bit of stick with a string attached. I would put some corn on the ground under the riddle and get a way away and wait. Down it comes! I pull the string and it's caught under the riddle! I was a naughty boy! I had one pigeon with me one day in the van when I was doing my journey - I had David with me (that was before Pegler claimed that we weren't insured for passengers) and we hit another pigeon as we were going down a road. Well, we had that one, too!

Then there were rabbits. When I was at home I would take a dog with me, but I used to set snares as well. The best was harvest, when the rabbits got shucked up in the middle of the field and there were only two or three turns left for the binder. It was easy to catch them then.

Rabbits are best when they're young.

One place where they were safe was on the aerodrome just past Newnton - the rabbits would come out and feed while the big aeroplanes were coming up and down, and you couldn't go on the field after them.

Someone was having it on to me. They had a big dog, and a daft one. I said 'I want a dog that'll catch a rabbit' - one that would spring right at the rabbit and have it - because in those days you could be sent to prison for stealing rabbits. I didn't want a daft dog!

I've watched foxes, how cunning they are. They go a few steps and they turn to look at you, and go on, and turn round again. I took Edith to Shipton Moyne one day, the first time she came to Tetbury; you know you go to Shipton Moyne on the Bath road and you turn down to Shipton Moyne; on the right there is a wall, and a stile in the wall and you go across to Wormwell Lane - that's where Mother and Dad did their courting, in Wormwell Lane - and we went across to Wormwell Lane, and it was the first time she saw a fox, a live fox, in the field. It was real sly.

Not long after, I took her to Down Ampney, where my mate Bill was still living, and she cuddled a lamb. That was the first time she really met a live lamb, and she never forgot it.

You know what a seed-lip is, don't you? A thing that the farmer used to sow his corn? I always called it a zidlip, because that's what everyone called it. I was ever so surprised when I went into a museum a few years ago with Edith and there it was, a zidlip on display, and the sign said SEED-LIP. Well, of course I understood at once what it was and what the name was. But don't go calling it a seed-lip - it's a zidlip!

But I don't suppose you know that I have used one, and a fiddle as well? That's not the musical instrument. I expect you know what a sower's fiddle is. It was at Leighterton, at a farm where I used to deliver the baker's bread from Peglers; before that they grew the corn and ground it into flour and made their own bread. It was wonderful, real bread, not white, because you can't make bread white with that sort of flour with nothing in it, no bleach or anything; but most of their bread was what I delivered, at that time. Apart from that bread they were self-sufficient. They grew everything for themselves, and they used the seed-lip and the fiddle, and at one time they didn't bother with baker's bread.

Before they widened it Upton road was so narrow that there was only room for the young men to skip in the road. Skipping in the road sounds ridiculous now, but the first thought is that the young men had no money to spend, either because their fathers got a wage but it all went, or they were married and all their wages went on the family. If it hadn't been for growing vegetables I don't know how they could have existed. When Alec Price used to come home on leave he would go skipping with the other young men in the road, and he would play with us, too. My brothers and I were too young, but Hector Walton, Reg Boulton and the Medcroft boys were all eighteen at the same time, and they had nothing. Anyway, they used to go skipping together. All of them would jump in while the rope was going round.

Young men in the army or navy coming home for leave during the war would play skipping in the road.

As well as skipping with a big skipping rope they played other games: we had a hiding game we played that we called 'first back' when all but one person had to go and hide and get back to the post before the other fellow, and if they did, they beat the man. We had a lot of fun because there were plenty of places you could hide. You could get into a tub in Walker's yard or anywhere. If you could get back when you had been spotted you were real good. Even better, if they went past you without spotting you, when they had gone past you could creep out and then dash back and beat them.

You see, we never had a copper to spend, and young men who were working had nothing because they had a family. By about half past nine in the summer it would get dark, and there were no lights anywhere, and we would play the parcel game and get hided: we made up a parcel with paper and string, and tied a long string to it, and left it in the middle of the road and waited for someone to come along. When we played the parcel game it was always getting dark and we could be behind the railings. Nobody could see us. Somebody would come. My mother was one of the first to be caught. She saw the parcel lying in the road and went over to it and picked it up, and it was pulled straight out of her hands on the string! It scared the life out of her.

And young men did other things like stealing people's front gate - tom foolery. But you see, people didn't have money for entertainment.

In the morning when Dad went to work he would turn round and check that the gate was shut. He always shut gates and doors after him. That's what he was like.

Once someone took our gate and Fred Walker split on them. He told Dad. He was their friend, and he would have been with them. Dad never said anything at all about it, but he never liked Fred Walker after that. Anyway, the gate came back.

You know we had a band in Upton Road, with all sorts of instruments, especially a drum. It was a piece of tar barrel with a string to hold it round your neck. We marched up and down the road with the band playing. Hector Walton was a bit older than me, but he was in the band with me. His job was hitting the tar barrel. Hector was as soft as I am.

Another thing you used to see often was whip tops, the tops coloured with crayons to see them go round, but that was mostly schoolboys, not young men with jobs.

We had some good games. You see there was no traffic. There was knocking on the door and running away when someone came to open it, and one of the best - another one to play when it was getting dark - was to fasten one door to the next one with a bit of strong black cotton. Then you knocked on one door and get across the hedge and waited for someone to come out. They would find that there was nobody there and shut their door. That would make next door's knocker go and they would come out to see who it was. There'd be nobody there, and they would go in and the first door would go again! We enjoyed that! But one day a man was waiting for us and he came out and chased after us. Well, as I was being chased I lay down in the gutter - remember it was quite dark - and he ran past me. The advantage of having no lights was when I dropped down in the gutter! The man was mad, he was after me and the other boys, and he couldn't see me in the dark.

That was when we were playing up London Road, beyond the gasworks. Oh ho ho, I had to run!

Going to work so much stopped the gallop of enjoying myself, but this was something: at Avening there used to be what they called the fly. That was a trap. It had two big wheels right at the back. It used to go to the station at Tetbury from Avening and bring people back. It was only passengers. He could get four people in it. The driver was a big man and he sat up on the trap with a long whip in his hand. Now, as boys we wouldn't notice it until it had gone past and then we would leap up and hang on. You see, the people in it were ahead of the wheels, so you could get up on the back spar.

Then some other kids would see you and they would shout 'Whip behind you, Mister!' and he would try to get you off the back of his trap with the whip.

We had some nice days. We had a gay life!

– THE EIGHTH PART –

The Rest of my Career

After The Grey House, Milward's shoe shop and Wright's paper shop I got the job of errand boy for Gale's; then I got a job working at Pegler's bakehouse. After that I left school and I went to work for him full time.

But the day I left school I didn't go to Pegler because I knew I had another job to go to, at Pike's garage in Hampton Street. I don't think Mr Pike was one of our relations. I went to see him and he gave me the job. On the Saturday I went with Mother and we bought two pairs of mechanic's overalls. They cost her half a crown - two and sixpence. I turned up at Pike's early on Monday morning and he said, 'Oh, we don't want anyone now!' I don't know whether I would have been any good working in a garage, but I didn't get the chance. I was always an unskilled man!

Well, after that I got the first full time job, working for Jim Pegler, back at his bakehouse in Long Street, and I became a baker. That was my first real job, and I went there because there weren't many jobs to be taken. Harold Major was a lad then and he was working there already. There is a story about Harold: he stole some sugar from the bakehouse and got forgiven, and then I got some sugar given to me by Gilbert Pegler to say, Don't steal it! He was a right funny lad was Gilbert.

When I had finished work at Peglers I used to run home from there to our house while the chimes were being played. I didn't stay there very long that time, because I was soon sick to death of Mrs Pegler, but of course I went back there, twice. I couldn't stand Mrs Pegler's loud mouth and grumbling. She was never satisfied, though she could be very kind as well.

When I left Pegler the first time I worked for the Pellys at The Priory, doing all sorts of jobs for hardly any money (I never told Pegler that!), but mainly helping the gardener, collecting weeds and rubbish and so on.

I started work there, at The Priory, at eleven shillings and sixpence a week. That's what Pellys paid me. Then it went up to twelve and six, then fourteen shillings, and I was earning fifteen shillings a week there before I went back to work for Pegler.

The best part was when we went to Westonbirt Show at Westonbirt House. That was a bit of a laugh! We went to the show and one of the Westonbirt gardeners was there while we were looking at one of the exhibits. He said to me, 'What's that flower?' and I thought he was joking, because it was just a flower that everyone knows; but he wasn't. I said 'Why, you ought to know!' but he didn't. Anyway, I had to tell him. It was a bulb of some sort - I can't remember now.

I used to go to the Westonbirt bothies after that with bread. The bothies were a row of very small houses. Several men lived at their gardens, you see. There were a lot of men working in the gardens there at that time. Rene was courting one of the gardeners but it came to nothing. I don't think you would have any idea what a big garden like that was in those days. They were said to be twenty-five years in advance of everyone with bulbs.

My cousin, Alfred Vizor, Fred Vizor from Crossroads at Shipton Moyne was the butler at Westonbirt House before it was a school. Everyone called him 'Buttons'. And when it became Westonbirt School I always supplied them with bread, tons of it over the years. I came to know the bursar there well. I've supplied the man with loads and loads of bread. Since then my brother Eddie worked for him, too - that is, under the man's jurisdiction.

One of old Mr Topps the baker's sons, who was a funny man, was courting a girl then in one of the houses at Westonbirt School.

I liked the job at The Priory all right, but I'm not earning much. So I went and got the other job, back to Pegler again and stayed for a few years; and then I left them again, for the same reason as before.

I was out of work. I had nothing to do. I bethought me to go sweeping chimneys, so I did that. I had all the equipment and a motor-bike with a long box like a sidecar to carry it all in. I bought the business from Harry Underhill. He was an old man and at first he used to come out with me until I knew what I was doing - that was in the deal. At first I did quite well, because we went to the big houses - for instance, at Upton Grove, Squire Harding's, we used to get a pound straight away for doing the chimneys - a day's work. I had clients that Harry introduced me to: 'This is the new sweep!' at Easton Grey and Boxwell - all the big houses. You had to climb into some of the old chimneys. At Boxwell when we first went in I remember there was a table laid for us for our breakfast - we began work early - and we began with two eggs each, except I had three because I had one of Harry's. And the master said to Harry 'I am going to tap a barrel. Don't go without!'

I'll tell you one thing about Harry Underhill: in the Spring he and his wife would go out into the country and pick every dandelion they could find, to make wine.

I used to do all the big houses, from Easton Grey, in a big house by the river, to past Avening. The first time I went to Easton Grey, Holborow was working there.

I mostly went to the big houses, but once I went to a farm at Chavenage and the farmer and his family had gone to the market. One of the girls says 'Would you like a glass of cider?' and I said 'Yes.' I sipped it while I was working, and it was very nice. I had finished the chimney, and I was putting everything away, when she came back in. 'Will you mind finishing the cider?' she said. 'I'm expecting them back any time. I don't want them to see I have given you a drink.' So I drank all the contents straight down, and I went off to my bike and put the tools in the box, and I got on and I rode back to Tetbury. I don't know whether it was particularly strong cider or whether it was because I drank most of it down in one go, but I was so drunk! It was all I could do to get back, but of course the roads were empty then. I went to Wisteria, to the pump house, and I lay down on the box attached to the bike and I slept.

At Westonbirt Lodge when I was doing that job I knocked a bat down. It was dark and there was nobody there and no furniture at all, and the bat came out and fled around the house. It knocked my candle over and put it out and I hit out with whatever I had in my hand and knocked it down. It was on the ground, and I picked it up. Afterwards I stunk! Oh dear, I think they're horrid looking things. There used to be a lot, far more than you see now; my Pike cousins used to throw their hats up in the air and catch them.

When I was sweeping I always kept myself washed and clean. I would get washed as soon as I got home - in a bowl of cold water from the well, of course.

After that motorbike was when I had my first car. It was an air-cooled Rover, the most comfortable car you could get. I paid £8 for it to Mr Gale when he came up in it from Lands End. He was a very good salesman. He had a motorbike then, and later he gave me a list of places to buy petrol and to say 'Mr Gale sent you.' And it was right, you know, because right down to Cornwall they would say 'Mr Gale? Oh yes, come in!' Everyone in Cornwall knew him. He must have been a decent fellow, mustn't he? He brought the car up from there, and I used it in my chimney sweeping. But in the end the car fell adrift, like anything does. I sold the tyres, and Dad made the hood to cover the garden seat. That was the end of chimney sweeping.

When I started as a chimney sweep I had plenty of work, but in a short while people were altering their fireplaces and there was less for a sweep to do. Even we had a new fireplace put in at Upton Road. The only places that did well were the gentry's houses. For instance Upton Grove, Squire Harding. A pound a time. These were big chimneys. I used to climb up them. But it came to an end.

And that brought me to working for Charles Hedges the builder; and as Gilbert Pegler had taught me to drive I got to look after the lorry for him, going for a load of sand and then gravel at South Cerney. There was one great big pit there then. It was well used. I knew the person who owned the pit. Like Charles Hedges he was in the Meeting, and he made a lot out of it. I believe he owned the land before they began to get the gravel out.

Another thing I did, whenever I could, was to take all the accessories out that the workmen wanted where they were building. And Mr Hedges would send me to Bristol or Stroud or anywhere on errands, like fetching a load of stuff, cement or wood or whatever. Often it was bricks, or sand or mortar. Anything! There was a cradle on top at the front, over the driver, so that you could lie the ladders upright. I used to go to Bristol and go round the shops for him and bring everything back. Once they loaded it so much at the back that all the way back to Tetbury the front wheels kept lifting off. But I got back.

One time I met another lorry driver on a hill when we stopped for a break, and he saw that I was from Tetbury by the writing on the lorry. He said 'Hello.'

I said 'Hello, Mr Lea!'

'How do you know I'm Mr Lea?'

'Well, he looks just like you. You must be his brother. You're exactly like him.' And it was the brother of Mr Lea from Tetbury, and he did look exactly like him, and he asked what his brother was doing. He wasn't going to Tetbury.

Then I took all the stone to build a gentleman's house at Westonbirt. All the outside stones were what they call shaddies, that is, they were cut like bricks. The actual builder was a man from Chippenham and he was so pleased with me he asked me to bring back a load of pudlock holes next time.

'Excuse me?' I said. I had no idea what pudlock holes were. 'You want me to bring you some holes? Holes?' I didn't know what they were but I was too fly to fall for anything about a load of holes. Anyway, then he gave me two bob!

I went with the lorry to Cirencester too, where Mr Hedges' mother and father lived.

When there wasn't any driving to be done and when I had the chance I could do some gardening for Mr Hedges. He had a garden behind Joneses on Bath Road, next to the quarry, but he didn't do anything to it himself and I could dig it for nine pence an hour. Once I found some lettuces growing there that nobody had planted, and I had them!

How I got my next job is a bit complicated. I went to work at Down Ampney. It's near Cricklade, past Ciren. I went to work as a baker for a man called Mr Herbert, in the Exclusive Brethren.

When I finished chimney sweeping and driving for Charles Hedges I was out of work, and through friends at Cirencester or South Cerney I heard talk there was a job going at Chedworth, as a baker. Chedworth is where my sister Irene, Rene, went to live with our uncle and auntie - Mr and Mrs Alfred Vizor. They kept the Waggon and Horses there. That's why Rene isn't on many of the photographs of the family, because she wasn't living in Tetbury, she was living at the Waggon and Horses, and working there, of course. Well, I used to go there on my bike.

Anyway, I heard that a man was going on holiday, and they needed a baker for a short time, to fill in just while he was away. He was Mrs

Woodley's son. So I went to Chedworth and did the job. And I was coming away, to go back to Tetbury, and I thought I would call at Down Ampney to the Herberts. I didn't know them very well but I knew they were in the Meeting at South Cerney - sometimes Mr Pegler took me there when he was preaching, when I was working for him. When I got there they were talking about making a new oven. They said 'Why don't you stop with us for a bit?' And I did. I didn't go home. They asked me to stay a week, and I stayed much longer.

The mother, Mrs Herbert, was the baker. The father was interested, but his wife was the baker. He was a funny man. But still, he was all right.

When I went to work for Herberts it was different altogether from Pegler's. When you were baking there wasn't a place for the fuel. You put your two faggots of wood - ash if you could get it, that was the best - straight into the oven when you had finished baking and when you came to bake you set fire to the wood, and you shut the door and because it had been in a hot oven it burned straight through, Whoosh! and you let them burn right away so that there was hardly anything left, but the oven was white hot and like flint. Then you took a sack and wetted it in a bucket of water and wrapped it round the stick of the peel, and then you swept it out. You wiped round the inside of the oven with that to take out any ash there was left, though there wouldn't be much left; then you laid the loaves in on the floor of the oven with the peel and left them there to bake slowly till they were done. It took about three quarters of an hour for a batch of large loaves and a bit less for the smaller size, but not much. And we had a little lamp that stayed in the oven, lit, so that you could see that the bread was done - it was like one of those Roman ones in the museum, an oil lamp, just a pot with a spout and a wick. There was a lot of hard work.

We used to go to the Meeting at South Cerney in Mr Herbert's car. I remember one day the wheel trim of the car came off on the way. I am told that Reg Cleaver used to go and preach at South Cerney sometimes.

There were a lot of cows in Down Ampney. I knew a man who looked after hundreds of cows, a big man, but I can't remember his name now.

Gilbert Pegler's brother Reg lived in Cricklade at that time. He was the baker of Cricklade and he left the baking trade and got a job and was satisfied with it too: he said 'That was the best thing that I ever did.'

When I was working for Mr Herbert there were two young brothers, Joe, and Jack who was my friend. One other brother was called Phillip. They called him Phillip, the lover of horses. There was another boy that I called Fred, but his real name may have been David. I don't know any more about him. There were two sisters. One of them, Grace, died early. She worked in their shop in Fairford where they sold bread and stuff, and when we went round she took what she wanted off the cart. The Herberts had a horse and trap to deliver bread and cakes, and later they had a motor van. But when I was working for them, and saw the oven built, it was still a trap, drawn by an old horse that was blind in one eye.

Phillip, lover of horses, used to drive the trap. Sometimes I went with him. He was only a boy. He would stand up when he was driving and say 'How about that, Frank?' But one day a noisy lorry came along and the horse saw it with its good eye and stopped dead, just as Phillip was doing his trick.

Two of us who worked for his father were sleeping in single beds. The other fellow was my mate. His name was Bill Coldrick. He married the Herbert's other daughter, Mary, and for a time he was the manager of the bakehouse, but he died. The Coldricks were a nice family, and his brother's name was Fred.

Jack wanted to be amongst the men. Jack would be younger than me, but he wouldn't be too young. He came in the bedroom in his little shirt. He said he wanted to sleep with us. 'Well,' I said, 'you can't. We're sleeping in single beds and there's no room for you!'

'Can't you push the beds together?' he said. So we had to push the beds up together so that he could come in, in the middle. Jack, that's who I'm talking about, would get in between us.

Jack Herbert was a real nice lad. See, those kind of things happen: Jack had all these ducks and he gave them to Joe because they never did any good; they started laying as soon as ever he gave them away! Our Raymond knew everybody, and one day not long ago when he had moved to Stroud he met the eldest daughter, Mary. She was living there, too. Well, of course I should have loved to see her! Because they were so nice, really nice! I won't know anything about it now, because Raymond's gone. You know how people get scattered around. It is funny when you go to find somebody - we could have had a laugh, couldn't we?

I have heard that Phillip Herbert is still with the Exclusives. He doesn't speak to his family. He would have to speak to me, if I saw him. I would like to go into his baker's shop and ask him for two pennorth of stale push (that's yesterday's pastry).

When the new oven was done, the Herberts were all right and they didn't need me any more. But I was there a good while. And what their children said was: 'What a grand time we all had!'

I would have liked to know about Mr Herbert in later years. I never had any chance to meet the Herberts when they came to Tetbury later (because they used to come to Tetbury). They had a baby grandson at the same time as our Elizabeth Ann was born, and in the Maternity hospital too, at the top of Gumstool Hill, that used to be the Workhouse. It's rather interesting.

It's ever so funny, I almost met Joe when I was with Elizabeth Ann, when I was looking up at the swallows at Bourton on the Water. They were just up in the eaves.

He had his daughter with him. We were all on holiday at the time, about 1950. He came up to John and David and he said, 'Excuse me, are you with that man, and is he Frank Peters?' John told him it was, and then he told me, and I saw Joe. But he went off and didn't come and speak to me. Isn't that funny?

Anyhow, for a short time I was working at Down Ampney. Then I went back to Tetbury. Then in 1930 I left Tetbury because I was out of work again. But one thing I did before I left: when the dentist came to Tetbury, to Shepphard's barber's shop in Long Street where we got our hair cut for twopence, I went to him and he did my teeth. He pulled them all out, and I have had false teeth since then. I was twenty four.

Down Ampney was the last job I had in Gloucestershire, except for the years from 1941 to 1947 when I worked for Pegler again. After that I always worked in Hull till I retired.

But here is a story about when I was working for Clark and Clark, at their bakehouse: there was a woman who made fish rolls next to their bakehouse; she left them outside for a bit, and a dog came along and weed on them. She didn't know, but I did.

I stopped being a baker when one of my 'brothers' in Hull gave me the sack and after that, as I said, I worked in a sulphur mill until I retired. It's a funny job, isn't it? Well, there's tons of it. There's tons of it. It's a lifetime, isn't it?

My friend Jack Herbert took this photo of me with his brothers and sisters in the garden behind the Down Ampney bakehouse.

– THE NINTH PART –

Away from Tetbury

SHIPTON MOYNE RELATIONS - PETERS AND VIZOR

Mother and Dad came to Tetbury from Shipton Moyne. My mother was Amy Vizor. Her family lived at Crossroads at the corner of Wormwell Lane and had lived there for ever. All her brothers and sisters had names beginning with A: Annie, Arthur, Alfred, Alice, Albert, Agnes, Aaron and Austin.

Mother's family, the Vizors, lived at Crossroads in Shipton Moyne, on the corner of Wormwell Lane. Amy Vizor met Arthur Peters when he moved to the village and they both went to Shipton Moyne school.

Amy was born at Crossroads on 6th February 1870. She was the eighth child of Joseph and Sarah Ann Vizor. My grandmother's name was Elliott before she was married. Crossroads was a smallholding, and they had a lot of pigs and their own variety of peas, but Grandfather Vizor was a well-digger. He used to construct them and line them with tiles. He always called me 'Richut'.

Grandfather Vizor came downstairs every morning and the first thing he did, he went to the barrel and drew a glass of beer and drank it. He always wore strings or straps round his trouser legs. He called them his 'yorks'.

Joseph Vizor the Shipton Moyne well-digger, my other grandfather, with his son Albert the coastguard and my cousin Ellis. Wherever Uncle Albert was stationed he always came back to see his family. He often brought his children with him.

My father was Arthur John Peters. He was born at Upway in Dorset on 3 February 1871, the same birthday as Edith. He was a year younger than Mother. His father was Richard Peters, and his mother was Jane Otter. She was an orthodox Jew and her family cut her off. After she died, he married again, another Jane; my mother used to say 'Your Grandmother was a lady,' and she wouldn't say that about my Grandfather's second wife.

Grandfather Peters was a carpenter by trade. Richard and the first Jane Peters and their family came to live in Shipton Moyne, at the Thatched House, when he got the job as estate bailiff, the overseer with Estcourt House, and that's how my mother and father met.

My grandfather, Richard Peters, came to work at Estcourt House as carpenter and estate supervisor. He was living with his family in Hereford then, but he and my grandmother came from Dorset and Dad was born in Dorset, too. We called the water the Fishponds.

My grandfather had a good job with Estcourt House and got on well. It was a big affair, quite industrial, and he was in charge of all these things on the estate. It was a big job he ran. He used to design buildings for the estate. One thing he did that you can still see: he was the architect of Malmesbury Post Office, too. How that came about I have no idea, but that's what I always knew.

Arthur and Amy both went to Shipton Moyne School. This is my Dad's story. My father was disobedient at school. He must have been a naughty boy. But he wasn't a nasty man. The story is about Canon Golightly, the vicar of Shipton Moyne. He was the boss of all around there. He came to the school and he fetched out my Dad, and he gave him a lecture. I don't know what it was for. Arthur may have been being chastised but there might have been something wrong. Canon Golightly leaned on his walking stick and he kept on rolling it in the ground and digging a hole, and when he had finished my Dad got down and spit in the hole. That's the story. That's all I did know. That was the truth of it.

My Dad got a job with Mr Witchell at Tetbury when he was thirteen and he used to go to work on his bicycle. The interesting thing is that it was a wooden bicycle. Later he had a penny farthing, and when it was worn out we put it against the hedge at Upton Road to keep animals out. He began work on the 9th January 1885, just before his fourteenth birthday, working for Witchell the ironmonger in Tetbury Church Street. He was apprenticed to work in the ironmonger's shop for two years, and then in the workshop at the back, and of course I remember him working there as Witchell's blacksmith, with men working under him.

This is known in the family as the old black photograph. The soldier in the middle is my father's brother, the one they told me was lost in South Africa.

Uncle Harry, Dad's brother, went to New Zealand as an emigrant before I was born. He never got married. Like Dad, he lived at Shipton Moyne with his mother and father until then. There was another brother, too, who died in the South African war; they used to tell me he was lost there and of course I never met him. There is a very old, black looking photograph of three soldiers in uniform, and one of them looks like my Dad, but it wasn't. It was his brother, the one who joined the army and went to South Africa for the war there.

A lot of people from that part of the world, especially from Malmesbury, went to New Zealand or Canada, probably because there weren't any jobs at home. Uncle Harry got a good piece of land, and when he died he left us some money, but the bank made their money out of it first. Edith wrote to the Auckland constabulary and they wrote back saying we were 'indeed' entitled to it. We got forty pounds and spent it on our new chairs, the poorest you ever seen, comfortable, but come apart and split.

My other uncle, Walter Peters, was a blacksmith. He went to live at Pewsey in Wiltshire, but he belonged to Shipton Moyne, of course, and he had been apprenticed to Witchell like Dad before he left home, and worked with him there for a time as a blacksmith.

I remember when he came to see us and I was very little, though I don't really know him well. Uncle Walter's wife died in his arms. She was a baker and they had a shop. I went to see them once. He was a funny old man was that.

They had two daughters called Lydia and Queenie. Now, Queenie was a funny case and she had a funny life, actually. She came to stay with us once, and she put it on with Mother when she was at our house. She was quite young, younger than me. I don't think there was much in it, but she thought she may have offended Mother in some way and she made a fuss and put the blame on herself. She did some muttering. I always remember one of the things she said: 'Serve her out for it!' Another was: 'Hit me, Grandma, with that brush!'; people tell me another was 'Put that down, Queenie!' She was a silly girl. I think Lydia got married and went to live out in the country by Devizes.

I had a lot of relations in Shipton Moyne, mostly called Vizor. I think only my cousin Lily is left now. She still lives at Crossroads. At one time there were several Vizors in Tetbury, but the people who were supposed to be relations weren't called Vizor.

There was Mrs Poole, who lived in the little house behind the Bath Road Meeting Room before Mrs Kidd. I know her father was Cuckoo Walker. Her mother may have been a Vizor.

I'm not sure if Mrs Vick the butcher's wife was a Vizor.

Then there was Mrs Taylor, the mother of Mr Taylor who kept the sweetshop on the corner of Silver Street and the Market Place. She may have been a Vizor, too.

Mother had a lot to do with horses when she was a girl - she had her own horse at one time - but after she left school she got a job as gate-opener at Highgrove, and there was a little lodge that went with the job. Mother and Dad got married on 7th May 1896 at Shipton Moyne, and they went to live in the lodge. That was where their first child, Mabel Sarah, was born on 7th November 1897. Mabel died and they went to live at number 3 Upton Road.

Annie Cox was my mother's eldest sister. She was born at Crossroads in 1854 and after she married she lived at Bagpath until she died in 1943.

Aunt Annie was my mother's oldest sister, much older than her. She was born with a birthmark of a strawberry on her back. I used to deliver bread to Bagpath, you know, and that was where my Aunt Annie and Uncle Edwin Cox used to live in a beautiful house, very nice. He used to work on a farm. In the place where they ate there were always two half pigs against the wall - half a pig hanging here and half a pig hanging there. When he died she moved to a little house at the bottom of the hill.

I could go through all her whims. She would go out of the house with her key in her hand, cautious as could be: she looks up the bank; makes sure nobody is looking; and hides the key under a stone in the middle of the garden.

She would look at next door: 'Is Missus back [that's the lady next door]? No, she's not!'

'How do you know?'

'No fire!'

Aunt Annie's house had nice clean water - all Bagpath had water. There was a ram behind their cottage, in a field, though they couldn't get at it; but they had a spring of their own running constantly behind the house. They had a bath outside and the water ran into it.

The cottage was a big house that had an oven made with the house. It was built on the side, like an extension to the house: you got at the oven from indoors but you could see where it stuck out on the side. The oven was made with the house.

It had all been there for years but now it has been demolished. I used to drive down the hill with the bread - it was the last house at the bottom - but the last time I was there with the car I didn't think anyone could have driven down, and I got out and walked down the hill. But when I got down to the end of the road there was nothing there, as if it had never been.

Aunt Annie was 89 when she died, and they had a job getting her out: from that little cottage they couldn't get a hearse to take her body away. So in the end they strapped the coffin on to the luggage grid at the back of an old Ford car, and they went up the hill for the funeral that way.

This is where Aunt Annie lived at Bagpath. I went there a few years ago and I couldn't find the place. I think it must have been demolished.

They had a grandson called Edwin, too, who became a vicar. Someone told me he was the vicar of Maidstone in Kent.

In the summer Mother would hire a wagonette from Mr Vick the butcher in London Road. It was part of his job - part of his business, you might say. She would bring it up to the house and all us children would get in and off we went to see Aunt Annie.

Mother was the carter - she drove the wagonette. We would trot along. It was only six miles to Bagpath. When we got there, to the house at the bottom of Bagpath, she would turn the horse loose and let it go in the field next to the house, and we would spend all day there. When it was time to come back home she went into the field and made the horse come to her. When you watched her it was just like watching a man: 'Come on then!' she called. 'Come on, come on there!' She didn't have a problem making the horse come to her. She shook a bag at it to think she had some food for it (but she didn't) and it would come up to her and she got hold of it. And when she put the horse into the shafts she would be saying 'Up! Wey-ey! Back a bit!' and she got it tied up to the wagonette. I thought she was a clever woman!

When she had the horse harnessed up we would get in the wagonette and come home.

I had a cousin, Aunt Annie's daughter, who had got married and came to live with her husband in Northfield when he got a job at The Priory. She was much older than me, nearly as old as my mother I should think. I tapped on the door as I was doing my rounds, and she came to the door. 'How are you?' I said. 'What would you say if I asked to kiss you?' She was a bit startled, and she had never met me. 'Well,' I said, 'we're cousins.' And then it was all right, when I explained. At that time I used to go every week to see Aunt Annie at Bagpath, because I delivered bread there, but I had never met my cousin until then.

Uncle Arthur was Mother's oldest brother. He lived at Shipton Moyne, in a house about a third of the way down as you go towards the pub. Then he moved into the first bungalow on the left, nearly opposite his house. The house didn't have a water supply. They had nothing but a water butt outside to wash in. They had to get cold water out of the butt every morning of the year to wash their faces. That was all the water they had for everything. All my uncles and their sons at Shipton Moyne had a place outside to get washed, and they would splash and make noises, like men do, while they were getting washed out of doors in the cold weather.

Uncle Arthur always said one thing to the relations: 'Be you going to kiss I?' He was a labourer from the age of twelve. He was married to Eunice, a great Christian; my oldest sisters knew her best. I knew her sister too, actually: she lived in Brokenborough and I knew her there. When Aunt Eunice died I went to her funeral. Now that was when I was with the Brethren, and working for the Peglers as well. I wasn't supposed to take time out anyway, and of course I wasn't allowed to go to a funeral or a wedding or anything if it wasn't the Brethren. But I slithered off to it while I was out delivering bread and they didn't know about it.

Aunt Eunice had one long tooth at the top, on the right, and another long tooth that came up from the bottom over the top lip to meet it and covered the other. She was pretty good looking, only her face spoiled it. She was all right. Nothing was ever done about teeth in those days. The dentist in Tetbury was at Shepphards the hairdresser in Long Street - not in the barbers shop but on his premises, opposite Harrises.

I knew a lot more of our relations in Shipton Moyne. There were two girls, my cousins Nelly and Dinah, Uncle Arthur's daughters. They were a bit older than me, and Dinah was a WAAC in the first world war. She was a strapping girl, a big whopper, neither like her mother nor her father, but Nelly was petite. She was a thin person, as thin as a rail. Nelly married a postman and went to live past Ciren. Dinah got married and went to live in Scunthorpe, a place called Railway Cottages. I was supposed to go once and help in the bakehouse where Dinah lived - she didn't work in the bakehouse, but there was one there - when someone was on holiday, to look after the job. But it never came on. There was at least one more daughter, much older, but I never knew her.

Uncle Alfred was married to Aunt Elizabeth. I said he was the landlord of the Waggon and Horses at Chedworth, where my sister Irene, Rene, went to live with our uncle and auntie, and that's why she isn't on most of the photographs of the family, because she wasn't living in Tetbury, she was living at the Waggon and Horses, and later she was working there, of course. I used to go there and play bowls.

We went to see them once. I took my family to Chedworth a few years after the war, when our children were young, and they were very anxious that they shouldn't be seen in the pub, and they sent them straight through the passage and into the garden. My auntie was very worried because I brought them into the house. She said 'Take them all straight through! This is licensed premises and children aren't allowed!' I thought she was making a lot of fuss. Anyway, when Auntie found what Elizabeth Ann was called she gave her a doll, because she was Elizabeth Ann herself. I think that was nice of her. The house isn't a pub any more.

Aunt Alice went into service in Tetbury, working for Mr Paul the solicitor, and she became a cook. She got a job as a cook in London and met a Metropolitan policeman and married him. His name was Kilvington Carrick. I knew him when I went to live in Hull, because he moved to East Yorkshire, to Easington, and he was in the police force there. Very occasionally I used to go on the bus and see them there. He told me all his tricks: one was, there was somebody to be arrested, and he walked him to the edge of his division (this was in London) where the next beat began; and he would get rid of his prisoner there. They could get arrested by somebody else! That was so he wouldn't have to spend the day in court! Another trick was, for the same reason, he would go inside a gate until a known criminal had gone past, so that he wouldn't have to arrest him!

It's funny, I remember him but I can't visualise Aunt Alice now. My cousin, Amy Carrick, was a nice girl; there were two sons. Alan Vizor, Uncle Albert's son, who was my friend in Hull (though I knew him from

Tetbury and Shipton Moyne) used to give them rides on the back of his motorbike.

I don't know why, but Aunt Alice drowned herself.

My mother's sister Agnes I never knew. She died years before I was born, when she was sixteen.

Uncle Aaron was my mother's great friend and everyone liked him. He was a proper gentleman to his wife, who we called Aunt Shuck. She came from the end cottage at Easton Grey. I think she was a schoolteacher. They lived at Easton Grey and then at Cheltenham. The last time I met any of them was at my sister Olive's funeral. That was Phyllis, their daughter; you could tell she was a Vizor by her ginger hair. When the Vizors were living in Cheltenham, Phyllis worked at Melias, the grocer's, and Olive worked there too, in the same shop. Of course, they all knew each other and they spent time together.

Aaron became very ill with sleeping sickness after he had been abroad. He went to his sister, my mother, and she looked after him. She loved him. He was Mother's pet. Mother was so possessed by her brother she had him in her house and did her utmost for him, and he stayed with her for a time. Then the doctors wanted to put him in a home but his wife said 'I'm not having him in a home!' and she looked after him when he was so ill he could hardly move. She said to me after he died, 'He was a lovely man! I wouldn't let anyone keep him but me. He's been such a kind, wonderful husband.'

I went and stayed with them in Cheltenham once, when they had a business with plants. While I was there I helped Uncle Aaron to put a stake in the garden, a big post. I held it while he hit it, but he missed and hit my finger. It swelled up like a balloon and I had to go to the Eye, Ear and Throat Hospital where they had to cut it open.

I went running with Bob Vizor, their son, who was a racer, and I ran out of town with him, but I lost him because he got away from me. Bob was a dental technician by trade. He made false teeth.

Bob got married and he was a very old father. I mean he must have been quite old when he had children.

I hardly knew Mother's brother, Uncle Albert. He was married to Aunt

Alice, who was a Phillips from Tetbury, Gashouse Row, though I came to know her well later, when I went to live in Hull.

I remember a lot of things well, from when I was very little. For instance, one thing I remember quite well happened when I was in the pram, so I don't know how old I was, but I must have been young! This Vizor uncle from Shipton Moyne, that I have never seen apart from that time, Uncle Albert, who was Herbie's and Alan's and Ellis' and Lily's and Grace's father (I still call her 'Young Grace' though I suppose she must be eighty now), came to speak to me and he said a lot. He was dressed like a sailor - he was actually a coastguard - and he had a great big sword that he wore. I remember him coming and speaking to me in the pram. He was living at Cairnryan then, in the west of Scotland; I only remember seeing him that one time.

Some of Uncle Albert's family at Holmpton Coastguard Cottages in Yorkshire: my cousin Alan on the left, Herbie at the right; the tall girl with hair ribbons is Lily; the shorter girl is Edith Metcalf who used to play with the Vizor children. I went to Holmpton a couple of years ago and found the house and the Coastguard rocket station with the help of one of the neighbours there.

It was Edith who knew him and his family later when they moved from Cairnryan in Scotland to Holmpton in East Yorkshire where he finished his service. Uncle Albert gave Edith a pair of gloves once when she was a girl. She was all mixed up with the Albert Vizors. He died early, and when he died Aunt Alice went to live in Constable Street in Hull, and all my cousins lived there too. Later my cousin Herbie (Herbert) called his house in Hull Cairnryan. I met them again when I went to work in Hull.

Sometimes the Albert Vizor boys came to Tetbury for a holiday. Once when my cousins were staying with us I went off across the fields to Chavenage Lane with Alan. I don't think he knew much about the country. In the last field there was a pig - an old sow - and I wanted to keep away from her. But Alan said, 'Why don't you get on its back?'

I said, 'Because they snap - it'll bite your arm off!' He didn't know things like that.

Alan Vizor could be silly. When I went to Hull, once he was at Edith's house he was dancing in the front room and down went the aspidistra, smash on the carpet.

Of course they used to come to us in Tetbury and to Shipton Moyne sometimes. Alan's brother, Ellis, had heard me say about picking mushrooms, and once when he was about in Tetbury he asked me again, and I told him the best place, up Crudwell road from Long Newnton: 'Don't go down the Malmesbury road; when you see the sign for Crudwell, go down there...' and I told him to look out for such and such trees and he couldn't miss the field.

He went down there, and he found the road and the trees, and the place for mushrooms, but the boss was standing there in the field, and Ellis daren't go in.

Uncle Austin lived at Crossroads with Aunt Bessie and their children. Uncle Austin had one or two cows and heaps of chickens, and Aunt Bessie sold pigs to manufacturers. Out in the road was a strip of land and that's where the pigs were kept. They used to feed the cows on turnips, and the sheep had swedes. It was all good; they had locust beans too, those sweet things; they all went in the bag for the trough, because it was supposed to be good for them; and there was sainfoin grass, specially for sheep.

At Crossroads my Auntie Bessie always had a big piece of cheese, probably half a full-sized cheese, that's half a hundredweight of cheese. It was matured for two years before it left the place they bought it from and they put on the table at mealtimes and kept it there until they had eaten all of it and it was all used up.

Aunt Bessie's real name was Maud. Her father was Mr Wilkins. He was a dealer. He always wore a very big hat. He used to walk from Malmesbury to Shipton Moyne to see her at Crossroads.

They had their own variety of peas they grew, and they grew a lot of apples and pears in the orchard. They used to make their own cider - my father didn't like it. He said it was horrible.

There were several boys. Fred was the eldest cousin in that family and then Bill. They were two big strapping fellows. Bill used to milk the cows and turn the teat up and squirt the milk all over me. Bill went away and became a builder. But when we were little we used to play together. The Vizor girls at Crossroads were Lily and Maud and Bessie who died. I don't know how they all lived there. Maud married Bert Hoad and they went to live in Doughton. They had two sons, Leslie and Robin.

Bessie was an invalid. They put her on the wall and she kept everyone alive. Bessie Vizor was a magpie - a chatterbox. She would talk to anyone. They used to carry her to school because she couldn't walk. She was very intelligent. She was born when my brother Eddie was born. There was an article about her - I think it was in the Daily Mirror - when she died. I cut the piece of paper out, and I still have it. I carry it round with me in my wallet, and I always have.

When Tetbury Workhouse became the Maternity hospital Lily got a job as cook there. But apart from that Lily was greatly in demand at the houses of the gentry where they didn't have a cook any more; they would go to the butchers with her, and they used to pick out the joint, and then she would take it home and cook it for them. Or they would bring her to their house when they were having a dinner party, to do the cooking, and often she would bring great big lumps of meat back. They would have a piece of meat and only use it once. One of her customers was a millionaire and he would send his car to fetch her to his house. She wasn't in service - she provided a service from home. Lily stayed at Crossroads. She is 99 and still runs her own home, and although I had a lot of relations at Shipton Moyne there is only Lily now at Crossroads.

My cousin Fred, her brother, was the butler at Westonbirt House. He was a real smart man, good looking, too. In 1994 when we had the family party at Tetbury I was visiting Lily and this man came out - not a young man - and he said 'Excuse me, what are you doing here? What do you want?'

'Why, I'm visiting!' I said. 'Calling on my cousin Lily! And who are you?'

'Well,' he said, 'I'm her nephew.'

'Whose son are you?'

'My father was Fred Vizor.'

'Fred! Why, he never got married!' I said.

I hadn't heard anything about him since I went away. I left Tetbury in 1930, and I never thought he would get married then. Although I came back from Hull and was living in Tetbury from 1941 to 1947 I don't remember that anybody had relayed the news to me that he had got married. I thought he was like me, too old to get married, and he was older than me. This was Fred's son!

And nobody had ever told me that Fred had got married!

GOING TO MALMESBURY

When Grandfather Peters retired he went to live in Malmesbury, near The Triangle, and we used to go to see him there.

I knew my grandfather Peters' second wife when they lived at Malmesbury, on the slope as you go up to the Triangle from Tetbury. She was a tall woman. I remember her, but not my father's mother. They were both called Jane. First she and my grandfather Peters lived at Shipton Moyne and then they moved to Malmesbury.

When I was young we went to Malmesbury to see them and we would have stewed plums. We always had stewed plums there except when we had stewed rhubarb.

I don't remember him very well, but when I was very little and we would go there they would always put me to sit on the table by him; and he would sit on his chair and talk to me. Once he put his hat on my head - he said he wanted to see if I looked like him!

We had other relations in Malmesbury, Pikes, and we went there often. Uncle Charlie and Aunt Edith used to live down the hill from where the big mirror is, on the corner before you get to the Abbey. Uncle Charlie's sisters lived in Ingram Street where they had the seed shop. I used to like going to Malmesbury when I was very young because my cousin Ebby Pike used to work delivering bread with a barrow, a big basket on wheels, and I used to help him push it round the town. The bakehouse where Ebby worked then was in the same street as the seed shop.

After that Ebby worked for Ball's Bakery on the corner of Oxford Street. He used to deliver bread round Malmesbury. Then he had a proper baker's van with two wheels, and two doors that you opened to get the bread out. It had two handles and you pushed it. When I was a little bit older I used to like to go and help him push the van. It was like the one I had when I first worked for Peglers, before I learned to drive. Later, Ebby was a transport driver with the IMP. When he and his brother Bert went to live in New Zealand their mother and father went after them.

Ebby's and Bert's parents were Aunt Edith and Uncle Charlie Pike. Aunt Edith used to stay at home and make lace on a pillow. I don't remember Uncle Charlie having a real job. Uncle Charlie was a bit of a preacher. He was with the Open Brethren. He would go preaching, and he would go round to people's houses and have a meal. If it was near us he would come over and have a meal with us. The seed shop in Ingram Street belonged to my aunties and he was supposed to work there. Well, he slinked around there. He would work for an hour or two, packing up parcels of seeds, and then he would go out, slink off on the tramp to Tetbury and other places. I think they would be kind to him.

He couldn't stick to anything. He was always coming to our house for dinner. He was supposed to be a Christian, and he turned up at people's houses expecting to be fed! He came to our house pretty regular for his dinner - the five miles he had to walk to Tetbury was nothing to him. He would just turn up and my mother would feed him. It wasn't only our house where he went to be fed. When I was quite young and at work and he turned up I used to think to myself, I have to work like that, like a horse, and here he is, walking about like the King! Uncle Charlie turns up and gets a free dinner from my mother, and gobbles it all down!

Before the war Ebby and Bert used to come often to our house from Malmesbury on their bikes. They were a good bit older than we were: we used to entertain them by singing from behind the curtain. They wore caps (boys always used to have caps - they never went out without them) and they used to throw their caps into the air to catch bats, which were very common then, heaps of them, but I don't know whether they ever caught any.

Aunt Edith was Dad's sister. After they went to live with Ebby and Bert in New Zealand, if she corresponded with Dad she would write to him at Witchell's rather than at home. It never seemed the right thing, but there was nothing hidden. He always brought the letters home. I think she used to ask him to go to church.

When my sister Vera left and went to New Zealand to marry her cousin Bert I went from Tetbury on the train to Kemble with her. It was a sad night before. I took hard thought of what she said. She liked singing, and that evening she was singing 'Jesu lover of my soul'. Then she stopped, and she burst out crying: 'Where shall I be sleeping tonight?'

None of them came back again.

If you went to Malmesbury from Tetbury you had to walk unless you were lucky and met Reg Cleaver's father. He was the beer man and drove the dray for Warns. If you could, you would get a lift from him. Folk never had a ride, otherwise. My mother sometimes went to Malmesbury and she often walked, going to see Aunt Edith and Uncle Charlie; if I knew she was there I would trot there after work at night to meet her and walk home with her. I used to trot gently on until I got there. Sometimes I would go up the slope to the front of the Abbey and find she had gone the other side, round the back, and then I would have to follow her, still trotting, until I had caught up with her.

LONG NEWNTON

My sister Olive had married Fred Hills. They went to live in Long Newnton before they had the Post Office there and they lived down the bottom of the hill, at the farm house. Then they lived in a flat in Long Street, back in Tetbury. Then Fred and Olive moved back to Long Newnton.

Fred's auntie and uncle had the farm called Merchants Farm on the Malmesbury road a little bit past Long Newnton, more than a mile away from the house where Fred and Olive lived when they had the Post Office. Fred's auntie was his mother's sister, a Miss Brown.

Her husband was a big farmer and it was a big farm. The cattle lived out in the fields, but when they brought up the cows for slaughter they kept them in a yard full of straw. They couldn't move around and the yard got full of straw and cow mess. As the cows stayed in the yard for a time it got higher and higher. In winter it all froze and then they would cut it up and take it out into the fields as manure. There must have been some money!

Fred's father worked for them as a sawyer. The sawmill was part of the farm. They sawed timber in a pit, one man in the pit and one on the top, and that was how they managed to cut up whole tree trunks. It was a proper timber business, but that was all the machinery they had.

Fred got a job with Holborow's the builder, working with wood like his dad, but with real machinery. Holborow's built all the houses on the council estate behind Hampton Street. Fred had to do with all of them, and they were all built quite quickly, in one go.

One thing people don't believe is how dark it was when there weren't any electric lights. One night I went to see Fred and Olive when they were living at the farm house and it was extremely dark. When I was going home I went out and got on to the road and I found I'd left my gloves behind - they called out to me and said 'You've left your gloves!' They called and called, but I couldn't find my way and I couldn't get back to the house in the dark. I was already on the road, and there weren't even any signs of light from Tetbury because all the Tetbury lights were out (it was after nine o'clock, you see!). I had to go home without the gloves and go back to Long Newnton in daylight to get them again.

THE WIDER WORLD

There was an aerodrome at Leighterton in the first war and my friend Bill Maisey that I worked with at The Priory had a job there as a boy. He used to make the tea and collect sticks to keep the kettle boiling. He made a lot of money during the week and came home and had a bust-up every weekend. He was the spark in the town when they were all having fish and chips; all the boys wished they were Bill, because he had such a good job.

Uncle Austin worked there too, on the sewers during the war - just the water drainage - and he made heaps of money too. He never needed to have a paid job again.

This postcard was sent from someone in the Australian Air Force in 1917. On the back there is a comment about the state of Leighterton Road.

When they were building the aerodrome the road wasn't tarmac of course. In those days the roads were made of ordinary stone they dug out of a hole. It was like all the other small roads, only suitable for carts and horses. Well, the mechanism they used for building the aerodrome wore the road till it was over your ankles. The ground gave way. From the Tetbury National School all the way to Leighterton it was two big gashes in the road, up to the axle. Nobody would believe it now, would they? Later on of course they made a proper road, but when it was dry in summer in that day it went to dust and covered the hedges, all white. And the hedges were allowed to grow, like they aren't now. Then they got on to using small blue stones that they put through a screen, like a riddle, and watered it and rolled it. The roads were all tarmac afterwards, but not then.

When I wanted to go to Malmesbury to see my relations I would try to find someone, a farmer perhaps, going along the road in his trap. Then I would trot after him until I got there. I did a lot of trotting! When I was older and had a bicycle I went a bit further than Malmesbury, and sometimes I went as far as Ciceter (we often called Cirencester Ciceter then). One day I was going there with a few friends, and it was a hot day. One of the boys, Cecil Dickens, said he would go ahead of us because he could go faster, and set up the drinks for us at the Station Hotel just before the place where the road dips under the railway bridge, and he did. It was a bit silly. When we got there he had bought three pints of beer for us. But I hadn't had a chance to tell him that I didn't drink beer. It was because of my mother - I was always close to her, closer I think than any of the others, perhaps I was more like a Vizor in myself than the others were - I didn't know whether she would mind if I drank beer. I didn't ask her, so I didn't drink it.

The point of this story is that in Tetbury, especially before 1914, hardly anybody had any idea of anywhere outside Tetbury, and those of us who went as far as Malmesbury or Cirencester counted as quite well informed! Later I got more adventurous and went further. I first tried a car when I was still at school - a farmer said to me 'Can ee drive, Frank?' I said 'No,' and he said 'Get in and try,' and I did. But I didn't really learn until I was working for Pegler.

You might think, Well, there were always newspapers, and people must have read them. But in fact a lot of people didn't get newspapers; if they did it was the Wilts and Gloster Standard, and anything further than Stroud in that paper was a mystery. And of course there was no wireless and no television. I can't remember anyone I knew who took a national daily paper, though I delivered papers for Wright's shop for quite a long time. I never read a newspaper. We didn't always get the Standard in our house. The only thing I can remember that we always got was Answers. It came out once a week and my dad liked Mother to read bits out to him while he was having his tea.

There was no bus service to Tetbury when I was a boy. Then a bus started, going from Bristol to Cirencester. Then there was one from Tetbury to Stroud, later on, but I think it stopped again. Cecil Dickens got that job: he drove the Stroud bus.

THE CHURCH AND THE BRETHREN

I was always in the church choir at Tetbury. This is the view of the church I saw when I went back down Harper Street to paint boots at Milwards at lunchtime.

We were Church of England. I was in the church choir on Sundays, St Mary's. Of course, there's my big difficulty: I wasn't allowed to sing second part, because I was treble. I used to sing it all the same. That would be more to me than singing it the other way, you know what I mean. If you were a boy at Tetbury National School and you wanted to, you went into the choir. It was a Church school. If you were required for a service, they would let you out of school. Funny, isn't it? I used to go along with the rest of the boys and we had a cassock and surplice. It was all right. We used to sing for everything. This is one thing that has stuck in my mind: we had to make up when we were singing, like this: instead of singing 'Behold' we were made to sing 'Biff-hold, I bring you tidings of great joy'!

This is where we sang in the choir, in front of the altar. We wore black cassocks, surplices and white school collars.

Mr Street from the Long Street garage sang in a high pitched voice in the church choir. A lovely man he was, and a good singer.

We had a choir practice in the evening. When we went round the side of the church there was a tomb that had DIED WITHOUT SPOT on it. I used to think, That's all you know! A good lot of saints we were in the choir. I don't know why I left, I'm sure. It was automatic, I think. You got some coppers for going. We never had any other coppers! We never had any money at all.

The choir master, the music master, he had a tricycle. When we had the choir outing, to Weston Super Mare and suchlike, we went in a wagonette and he followed behind riding on his trike. When we got where we were going he would let some boys have a go on his trike.

We were all called Church of England. My sisters would go to church. My mother and father never went. He said he wouldn't go 'Because I can't hear!' You know, my father was actually a Jew, though I think he was brought up Church of England.

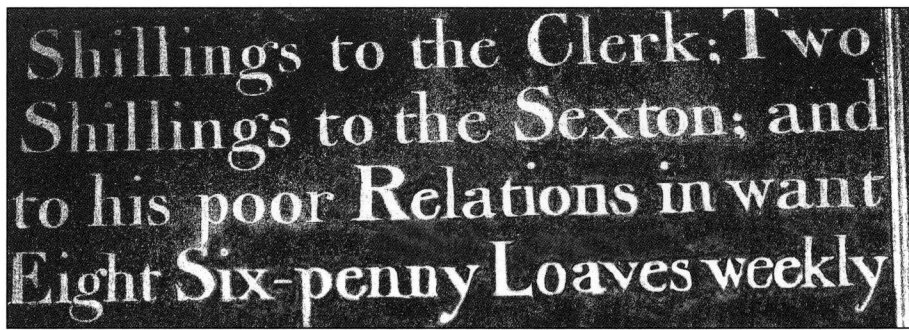

In the old days rich people left money for church charities. This is one of the charity boards in Tetbury church. When I worked for Pegler I baked the 'poorbread'.

St Mary's was supposed to be a pretty rich church. There were a lot of charities in Tetbury because people had left money to the church for charity. When I was a baker I used to go to the church on Saturdays and take the 'poorbread' - bread for 'the poor'. I used to make the bread myself. We Peterses were 'the poor' ourselves and we used to get two big loaves every Saturday, bigger than a quartern loaf, that cost sixpence each. Mother had a pair of sheets one year, and seven and sixpence another year, too. There were several charities for boots, and one for the men who got what they called a romsey, a hard-wearing coat for outdoors. Anything like that was a godsend.

There wasn't a Sunday School at the church, but we went to the Garret, the Open Brethren, in Long Street. We had to go somewhere. We children had to do what we were told at home and that's where we were sent. We were sent there because it was handy. I used to win prizes. I won a book, 'The boy that never lost a chance'. I never read the thing. I never had a chance to read it! I was always working. The prizes were for attendance and one thing and another. It was all right. A lot of Tetbury people belonged to the Garret. There was Mr Pitman, a tailor at Braine's and a Sunday school teacher, and Mr Wilkins, and Mr John Cook. Mr Cook was a lovely man. He was a baker for the same round as I did, you know, only different baker, Lewises, and different customers. Mr Wilkins was a butcher, related to Aunt Alice who married Uncle Albert and went to live in Hull. He worked for Butlers at the top of Long Street. I was at school with his nephew, Eric.

They called it officially the Long Street Room. One of the elders used to take the class, and he would bump them on the head with the Bible if they didn't behave! He was the father of one of my friends.

Mr Williams of New Church Street took this photograph. I think it is of the Open Brethren's recreation day, but I am not sure what year. I am sitting on the ground near the left. I am wearing a striped blouse, an eton collar (probably one of Hector's) and a hat.

Mr Pitman ran a cricket team for boys. I played in the Garret Sunday School cricket team, with Eddie and other boys. Some of the women helped. There is a photograph of some of us with Mr Pitman: There is Mr Pitman in the picture, and Bert Bignell at the left, then Stanley Wilkins and Eric Wilkins and Fred Maisey; then Edmund Peters, Leslie

Pritchard, Francis Peters, Charlie Crew and Wallis Pritchard.

Mr Pitman was a nice man and he was a good man. Once when we were playing cricket in the field in Blind Lane, Mr Vick's field, for the recreation day for the whole church, Mr Pitman hit the ball - of course, while he was playing with the boys - and it went into a lady's face. She was blind. That's trotting back a long time!

Mr Pitman had a son, Georgie, but I don't remember Georgie Pitman ever going to church.

Mr Pitman and the Open Brethren Sunday School Boys' Cricket team. Back row from the left, Bert Bignell, Stanley Wilkins, Eric Wilkins, Fred Maisey. Front row, from the left, Edmund Peters (Eddie), Leslie Pritchard, Francis Peters (Frank, me), Charlie Crew and Wallis Prichard. It wasn't a big team.

Now, when you go out of our house, at Upton Road, you turn right when you're going to Long Street, to the Meeting, don't you? And that's what we did, until we started being of an age to work, and then we were sometimes too tired, especially Eddie. Nobody watched us go off to Sunday school, and Eddie took to turning left instead of right. He had two Sunday schools to go to: either it was cars, or for a bit it was the Salvation Army. They gave him a beautiful uniform to wear, and do you know what he did? He sold it! I don't know who wanted it. He didn't go back to the Salvation Army after that: he went after cars or the Ormond's Head.

Now you know that I was working for Jim Pegler, who was in the Exclusive Brethren as people called them (not the same people as the Long Street Room where I used to go to Sunday School) and he had bought a van. Now, he would take me with him - he was the driver and I was his mate. That was not long after I had left school. One day we were out in the country delivering bread and we met a man who was on holiday with some relations that Jim Pegler delivered bread to. He didn't come from Tetbury. He knew Mr Pegler and he knew he was in the Brethren's Meeting, and he asked him if I was going to their church. He said, 'No.'

The man said 'I'm amazed!' While Mr Pegler was going on somewhere else, we had a little talk and I delivered my bit that I had to do. I was getting back in the van and he asked me 'Are you a believer?' Well, I couldn't say I was. 'Would you like to be?' he said. 'I'll ask you something. I've got a penny in my hand. Do you believe me?' Then he said to me 'Frank, why don't you come to our Meeting in Tetbury?' He asked me and I went. I suppose I was interested, too.

Well, to cut a long story short, I went there, and I stayed with them for over thirty years, and worked as a baker for several of the Brethren, after I left Pegler, especially in Hull.

Now you have heard me say that Mrs Pegler was a funny woman; but when I had started going to the Meeting she was kind to me in a way: after I had been working for a twelve hours' run, and I still had to grease tins and make dough before I could go home, she would give me a nice piece of cake and a cup of tea before I went on. When I had finished I used to come down the passage, not happy, and I used to think 'To whom shall I go?' and every time I used to left wheel and go up to the Market Place where the Brethren's chapel was. And the service went on until eight o'clock. I had to remember 'Thou hast the words of eternal life', and I hadn't had my tea - only the cake.

I have never resented it since.

Mr Charles Hedges was a big man. He was in the Meeting, and he had a milk business. He had **Tuberculin Tested Milk Produced By C Hedges** on the bottle. But Charles Hedges wasn't really a farmer, though he had some cows; he was a builder with his own building firm and that was his main job. He was a friend to me.

There are all sorts of stories about him. He had a dog and he gave it to his sister at Bicester in Oxfordshire. He took it in his car and drove home again; and the dog turned up at Charlton Road the next day. It had come all the way from Bicester.

His sister was married to Mr Herring, a grocer there; he had a shop with twelve assistants; and one time they arranged to take me to their house to have a holiday there. One day Mr Hedges' brother in law had to go to London on business and he took me in his car from Bicester to London with him. When Mr Herring got there he put his car into a garage and he had another car waiting for him with a chauffeur to make his calls in London. When they got back to his own car he asked the chauffeur 'How much do I owe you?' and the chauffeur told him.

'Why, it wasn't supposed to be as much as that!'

'No,' the driver said, 'but you wanted me to drive fast!'

I went to Bicester on my bike, but they brought me back in Mr Herring's car, with the bike tied on the luggage rack with rope.

One day when I was working for Mr Hedges he said to me, 'There's a big meeting at Cirencester tomorrow. Would you like to come?'

I said, 'No, I have to bring my sister home from Boxwell. I shall go over on my bike.'

He offered to lend me his car to bring Laura home. 'You can be there and back in no time and go to the Meeting!' It was a Morris Oxford.

I said 'I can't drive it. It's too big. I can't reach the pedals.' I mustn't have been very big in those days. But he put a load of builder's tackle, lifting gear, on the seat and I sat in front of it and drove it like that, and I picked up Laura and came back and met him again and we went to the Meeting together.

Sometimes I drove Charles Hedges' lorry when he needed a driver. He lent me the lorry, too, when Fred and Olive had to leave their first house at Long Newnton. 'Why don't you take your sister in the lorry?' he said.

I moved them and all their stuff to the flat above Lawn's hairdressers in Long Street.

Mr Pegler and Mr Hedges were both brothers in the Meeting, but Mr Pegler had a funny idea about Mr Hedges. He thought he was always being clever. But he wasn't - he was just good, and Pegler didn't understand that. Once he came to Pegler and asked if he could store some wood in the flour loft in Long Street. It was quite feasible. Mr Pegler said yes, he could - but he would still go backbiting afterwards. Mr Hedges wouldn't think anything wrong of Pegler.

One day long after I had finished working for Charles Hedges and I was delivering bread in the van for Jim Pegler, I was down near the Hare and Hounds at Westonbirt and I saw Mr Hedges standing in the middle of the road. I was coming, not from Tetbury but out of a side road, and crossing the main road. I wondered what was about. I stopped and I got out to see. I thought he was dreaming until I spoke to him. He said there had been a serious accident. He had swapped his Morris Oxford car with his sister's little car - not Mrs Herring - so that she could take all her family on holiday and they had had a crash. As they were going towards Bath a lorry was coming across, and she had put her foot down to stop it, but pressed on the accelerator instead of the brake. Morrises had the accelerator pedal in the middle in those days, between the clutch and the brake, and she wasn't used to it. When I got there the car and the lorry and the injured people - one was a very small child - had all been taken away. The child had been found down by the pedals. Someone had telephoned Mr Hedges and he had come out in his sister's car.

In the end he left Tetbury and went down into Somerset somewhere.

WHAT HAPPENED IN HULL

Now, the very first time I went to see my Vizor relations in Hull, I went there with Raymond for a holiday. We went from Tetbury to Gloucester on my motor bike and just parked it, and caught the train. The bike I had was a beautiful big powerful bike, a Ricardo. I didn't think of going all the way to Hull on it - I was too young and inexperienced.

We were going to stay with Ellis Vizor and his young wife Grace on Corned Beef Island, as they called it. It was a council estate. Ellis worked in Hull in the ticket office for the North Eastern Railway. Grace was a Clark; all the Clarks (who were bakers) married the Vizors (well, nearly all). Both families were in the Exclusive Brethren, and so was Edith Metcalf and her family.

At the end of the holiday Grace took us to the station where Ellis was issuing the tickets. When we left her and went to the train I thought, I've been relieved! I'm glad I'm going home!

The bike was still there in the street when we got back to Gloucester!

A few years later, in 1930, after I had finished being a lorry driver and a chimney sweep, and when the new oven was done and my job as a baker at Down Ampney had finished too, the Herberts were all right and they didn't need me any more. But I was there a good while. Then I went back to Tetbury, but I was out of work again and I went where there were jobs. In Newark in Nottinghamshire I worked for a baker who still has a stall in the market, and part of my job was to put up the stall and set it out first thing in the morning. I stayed with my cousin Lily (Uncle Albert's daughter) and her husband Philip who worked on the river barges. Another place I went to was Goole, in Yorkshire, and that is where I went to night school to get proper qualifications as a baker - I never got anything in Tetbury. There wasn't anything to get.

Then I was unemployed again and I heard through my relations that Clark and Clark in Hull wanted a baker (there were four Clark brothers who were bakers, and their mother and father and brothers and sisters were all partners). I came to Hull to get the job, and I lodged with Ellis and Grace again. By now they had moved to a little house in Chesnut Avenue (that's how you spelled it). That's when I met Edith.

You know, when I went to work as a baker in Hull I was in a room all week, working. I didn't see anybody in Hull except the people I worked with and the Brethren. I missed the country that much! Well, at the end of the week I thought, I'm going to the country! So after work on Friday I set out from the bakehouse down Newland Avenue, walking away from the city centre direction. I went down to the tram terminus and turned left. I had been walking for a long time and I came on a roadman sitting by a fire at the end of Chanterlands Avenue. I asked him, 'Excuse me, can you tell me how far it is to the country?'

'The country? You'll never get there tonight!' he said.

I was ever so disappointed.

But that was the time that I first met Edith.

I was already with the Brethren in Tetbury, and I quickly found out where the church was in Hull. On the first Sunday I went there with Grace and Ellis and as I was walking in I saw there was my auntie sitting with a young woman. The young woman muttered something to Auntie. What she was saying was (I didn't know at the time) 'Who is the young fellow clomping into the room?'

My auntie said to her 'He's my nephew, and he's not interested in girls.' That was true. I had absolutely no interest in girls.

After the service my auntie said 'Come to dinner with us,' and I did. The young woman was there as well and I was introduced to her: Edith Metcalf.

I met her again one day at the Ellis Vizor house when she came for a meal; there was a rush of young people there. Someone said 'Why not go for a walk?' and we all went out together.

One Sunday I heard all the Vizors were going somewhere, to Knaresborough, where the old woman lived in a cave, you know, on the next Saturday and I said 'Any chance of going with you?'

They agreed, and I said, 'I'll go along with you' - as a group, I meant.

And the young woman, Edith, was going with them, and so I said to her 'I'll see you on Saturday then.' That was all. She thought I had attached myself to her, and so did Ellis Vizor. He was a bit cast out. He had had his eye on his wife's sister for me, I think, and he warned me about Edith.

Apparently she was always rude about me, a country boy, to her friends, and years later she admitted that she had always called me 'Strawhair'. She also told me she had heard Grace say 'I've given Ellis Frank's food, but he won't mind!' I suppose I got something afterwards (in fact Ellis and Grace were a bit tight. I've seen one of them pick up the phone and say 'I wonder if I can afford to make a phone call today?').

But Edith wasn't a deceiver. She had had a boyfriend before, a baker who came from Cirencester to Hull, but she had given him up, and he went to work in Scarborough, and he married a woman there with some money. Well, that's how I met Edith. You know the terrible outcome? I married her! And from that time on we had a good life.

I'll tell you something. I had no love in me until then. I was ordinary, but the only love I had for anybody was for my mother, until I met Edith.

By the way, one Hull Vizor got away: Alan was going out with a girl called Evelyn, and one day he went with his family to a Brethren meeting instead of going out with her. She followed him in and dragged him out, and he never went back, and he married Evelyn. Alan died a long time ago but I still see Evelyn sometimes.

I married Edith in Hull, of course, because both us us were living and working there. My mother and father came to the wedding (Dad lost his glasses during the church service and kept muttering loudly 'Where's my specs? I can't find my specs!') and later they stayed with us in Hull. But then he died at the beginning of 1938, just before I knew Edith was expecting a baby. I wanted to tell him as soon as I knew, and I never did.

Someone telephoned to the bakehouse where I was working (it was in January) to tell me he was very ill. Of course, he had died. It was a heart attack, as he was coming along the flat stones from Tetbury along Upton Road, near Blind Lane. He hadn't been retired much more than a year.

We had bought a brand-new house in 1937; it cost us £500. In 1941, after our second baby, David, was born, I heard that Pegler wanted a man. We came back to Tetbury and I got a job with Pegler again. We lived in a house that Pegler owned, 6 Bath Road. Now they call it The Old Toll House. In 1947 Edith wanted to go back to Hull and I got a job as a baker with William Jackson, a factory baker, working shifts.

Several years later, when Mother was about 80, I thought I ought to bring her to stay with us in Hull. Edith's sister Ethel had had a stroke, and I used to take her and her husband Arthur down to his family home in Somerset once a year, and bring them back a couple of weeks later. We always stopped at Upton Road going and coming each way and I thought, Why don't I bring Mother back with me? But there wasn't time to write again, and of course not many people had a phone then. Well, on the Saturday we went down to Tetbury and stopped there for our dinner and I said to Mother - I asked her about coming back with me.

'Oh,' she said, 'I couldn't do that!' and I asked her again, but she wouldn't. Two of my sisters were there - it must have been Rene who lived next door and Olive came over who was living at Long Newnton, and they tried to persuade her, but no, she couldn't travel all that way in a car.

They knew I was coming back next day, and when I got there on Sunday Mother was waiting for me, packed up and dressed for the journey. They had been working on her!

She got in the car and I drove off gently. By then I knew every café and toilet between Tetbury and Hull, and I think we stopped at most of them. We came to our house in Hull and the car stopped. 'Wherever are we now?' she asked.

'Outside our house.'

'We never are! We haven't come as far as that!' But we had, over two hundred miles, and she spent a fortnight with us, and did a lot of sewing and mending sitting on the old settee on the lawn that I had 'reupholstered' in plywood and lino. She would have been bored with nothing to do, because Edith and I were both out at work then, and the children were all at school. She wanted something useful to do.

One of my favourites. I often look at this photograph Edith took of Mother in Hull and think of her, sewing and mending in the sunshine.

I had a lovely mother, bless her! I always think of her when I see her in that photograph, sitting in the garden sewing.

She stayed with us until it was time to bring Ethel and Arthur back on the third Saturday, and we went back to Tetbury.

Edith and I had our pictures taken after I went to work in Hull. This is the one I gave her.

MOTORBIKE AND SIDECAR

Now, here's something: when I first had a motorbike at home I kept it down the side of the house. That was a Triumph Ricardo. There weren't any more of them around. If it was here today and you put it out of doors it wouldn't rot - all the good metal on it.

I got my mother on the back. She only went about three quarters of a mile, and she shrieked and shouted. I think that was enough for her, but she went on it. There was no danger. She was bigger then than me! Mother didn't mind, but my dad didn't like it.

If my dad was in the garden when I went out, he would always be inside the gate, and he would creep out of the road. If he could, he would go in the house where he couldn't hear it at all if I had to start up. Dad didn't like motorbikes. He may have been a bit afraid of them, or maybe he was frightened to death.

I would have been afraid if I had had to do anything with horses, and he just used horses when he drove for Witchell; I suppose he wasn't familiar with motorbikes, and I wasn't familiar with horses.

There were some of the Cleaver lads, a family who didn't live in West Street, and I bought a motorbike and sidecar, an Enfield, a very old one, off one of them, Victor. I knew Victor's brother, too. That was a lovely bike. It had a handle in front of you, on the petrol tank, to change gear. In 1930 when I left home for another job I left the bike and sidecar behind. Eddie had the bike and looked after it, but I don't think he used it much. He was more a car man. Most people are.

I went back to Tetbury a year or two after I left, when I was working in Hull. I had met Edith there and I had arranged for us both to come to Tetbury for a few days and stay at Upton Road. I took her to Bagpath to meet Aunt Annie, and to Shipton Moyne, and so on; and I took her in the sidecar. It was all right. We went to Cheddar and Weston super Mare as well. We had a lovely time.

The sea was a mile away at Weston. We made a record on the pier. We couldn't understand it and we were talking all the time it was made. There's a lot of flipping rubbish on it.

Now, one day we were in Tetbury, up in the town with the bike, and there were two women there who came from Avening. They were both living at the top of the Market Place, a couple of doors apart, near The Crown, both married to the Cleaver brothers. They both had children. Victor Cleaver was with them. They were the family as I bought the bike from, and I said 'Hello, Victor,' to him and 'Hello,' to his wife and her sister in law. They both said 'Hello.' They looked at us, and then one of the women said, 'I know you very well, don't I?'

The other one said to her husband, 'Who is the gentleman?'

I said, 'Who brought you the daughter's cake when she was born?' because in Tetbury they always had a cake for a new baby, not necessarily for a christening. It was a cake for the birth, you see. This one was a christening cake. Well, I knew them very well indeed.

But she said straight off, 'No, it wasn't you, it was Mr Peters that brought the cake!'

I said, 'You don't know me, do you?'

Victor said, 'This is Mr Peters!'

When we had our first holiday in Tetbury I got my bike back from Eddie. Edith and I went out on it. I think motorbikes are lovely.

I think motorbikes are lovely. You're all open. But I wouldn't like one now. I'll tell you - the best thing was going across some water on a ferry. You can work your way to the front and go first. That's if they don't tell you to go such and such a place. But it was such an ordinary thing with me then, having a bike.

There's another story about that holiday in Tetbury when Edith came home with me: we didn't need all the sleeping room in the two houses by then, because the girls had all left home, and I slept back in number three; Edith slept in number four. One night I 'got on the phone to her' - I used Dad's speaking tube that I told you about, and I used the whistle; there was a whistle on the end of the speaking tube, all home made. I said 'Be quiet! There's a bird!' It was opposite, in the field, before they built the council houses. Do you know what it was? It was a nightingale. She had never heard one before, and I have never heard one since.

Mabel died when she was a baby and Vera went to New Zealand to get married. This is the last picture that was taken of all the remaining brothers and sisters: Clarence, Olive, Eddie, Rene, Laura, Raymond, Frank.

The Middle of Tetbury

- The Workhouse
- The Talbot
- The Fox
- Fox Hill
- Chipping Steps
- The Crown
- Silver Street
- The Green
- The Chipping
- White Hart
- Market Place
- The Jolly Butchers
- The Vicarage
- Church Lane
- Long Street
- Witchells Market House
- The Eight Bells
- Church Street
- St Marys Church
- Under Bath Bridge
- Baptist Church
- Warns Brewery
- Bath Bridge
- Grounds of The Close
- The Prince of Wales
- Harper Street
- Cottons Lane
- Blackhorse Hill